# *Daastan e Dastarkhā[n]*



Sadaf Hussain was one of the top contenders of MasterChef India in 2016 and is currently a consultant chef based out of Delhi. Sadaf grew up in Ramgarh, a small town in Jharkhand, and always dreamt of being in the food and beverage industry. An animator by training who worked in the development sector, his food journey took shape when he moved to New Delhi and chose to adopt travel as a lifestyle. An avid storyteller, he is passionate about exploring the background and origins of the dishes he encounters. Sadaf is a TEDx speaker, hosts food shows online and runs the popular food blog www.foodandstreets.com. He believes that everything and everyone has a story to tell, and lives to uncover these stories.

**Praise for the book**

'Sadaf is an honest and humble man. His approach towards food is about adding a pinch of nostalgia with some great flavours. This book is not just recipes but stories from his personal life that everyone can relate to. While reading, this book will take you back in time and serve you an awesome meal that you will not forget soon. In fact, it will bring you back to the book for more. Sadaf has a keen sense of flavours, and has these skills coupled with an unrelenting passion towards cooking.' – Kunal Kapur, celebrity chef and media personality

'This is a book that has been waiting to be written. I am delighted that Sadaf has undertaken this task with his trademark unpretentiousness, boundless curiosity and the knowledge of what makes a good story.' – Marryam H. Reshii, author of *The Flavour of Spice*

'Sadaf takes you on a memorable recipe journey to showcase the diverse cuisine of the Muslim communities in India. Make sure you're gorging on some Bihari Kebabs while you dive into this excellent read.' – Saransh Goila, celebrity chef and founder of Goila Butter Chicken

# *Daastan e Dastarkhān*

## Stories and Recipes from Muslim Kitchens

**Foreword by VIKAS KHANNA**

SADAF HUSSAIN

hachette
INDIA

First published in 2019 by Hachette India
(Registered name: Hachette Book Publishing India Pvt. Ltd)
An Hachette UK company
www.hachetteindia.com

SRD



ISBN 978-93-88322-41-6

Hachette Book Publishing India Pvt. Ltd
4th/5th Floors, Corporate Centre,
Plot No. 94, Sector 44, Gurugram 122003, India

Typeset in Arno Pro 11.5/15
by InoSoft Systems, Noida

Printed and bound in India by
Manipal Technologies Limited, Manipal

MIX
Paper | Supporting responsible forestry
FSC™ C043100

*You can't just eat good food. You've got to talk about it too. And you've got to talk about it to somebody who understands that kind of food.*

– Kurt Vonnegut, *Jailbird*

# Contents

# Foreword

Food has the power to connect different worlds, different generations and different cultures. My travels to different parts of the world have taught me a lot, and, more often than not, the dishes I serve all have a story within. As a chef, it is important for me to create a story on the plate and therefore, I'm constantly seeking tales to tell.

The beauty of a good food book is that one always discovers a new way to handle familiar ingredients. No matter how well you know a place or a community, there will always be someone who makes one dish differently in their kitchen, and has a unique style of narrating their stories. In this carefully curated book, Sadaf brings to light old recipes for a new audience from the Muslim community's culinary history, which is shown to be far more diverse than presumed.

I met Sadaf for the first time in 2016, when he was auditioning for the MasterChef India show. A determined man, he often surprised us with the dishes he presented, and always sought to improve his dishes with every review. I am delighted to know that after MasterChef Sadaf has forged his own path. His penchant for storytelling has ensured that he has injected the art in whatever he does – whether while cooking, presenting food shows or writing online. It is fitting that his first book is one of food stories.

Often, it is the light-heartedness of a shared meal or the memory of a great dish that we treasure when looking back on life. The beauty of a dastarkhān is that it is an invitation to share a meal, as stories are swapped after a long day. It is this sense of community that has been so effectively evoked and sets this book apart.

In these exciting times, when people are always ready to try something new, Sadaf's book brings to life old tricks of the trade and reminds readers of an elegant time, of slow-cooked dishes and elaborate meals. While we are used to sharing stories of ourselves around food, this is the story of food itself, and Sadaf has captured it in his characteristic style. His writing is simple and nostalgic, and this book is reminiscent of who he is as a person.

Sadaf has made an honest effort in documenting the stories and recipes, and maintains the romance associated with food through his mouth-watering narration. I hope this book inspires many others to document the stories of dishes from their own communities, because one should never take for granted these quintessential moments of life.

Chef Vikas Khanna

# Introduction

MY RELATIONSHIP WITH FOOD is beyond words. Ammi sometimes jokingly narrates two stories from my childhood, which hinted at an early attachment to food and my future career. When I was about two years old, my Nanna (grandmother) was giving me an oil massage, rubbing down my back. Usually, I'd cry during this process, but on that particular day she noticed I was quiet. What she hadn't realized was that I was silent because I was busy eating a chocolate I had managed to grab hold of. When she turned me over, she found me happily chewing on it. The second story has to do with why I liked going to school. I went, not to study, but because I'd get to eat three meals in the span of three hours between 7 and 10 a.m. In fact, I remember getting my first 'catering order' while still at school. Every 5 September, on Teacher's Day, we would bring snacks and cakes with us to school for our teachers. My first order came from my classmates; they'd asked for a sponge cake. I was very excited and together, Ammi and I made a half-pound soft and moist cake, and sold it for ₹50.

As my curiosity about food grew, I started spending more time in the kitchen watching milk boil, observing my aunts grind spices on the *sil-batta* (grinding stone), watching Baby Aunty, our house help, cook. The sound of food being cooked was music to my ears. Soon enough, I wanted to learn how to do it myself and this was my entry into the world of cooking.

I don't hold a degree in the culinary arts, nor do I have any professional cooking courses under my belt. My zeal to learn all I could about food simply led me to observe people and their mannerisms in the kitchen – how they chopped vegetables, stirred pots or put spices in a pan. I like calling myself 'khansama', which is the Urdu word for cook. I have learned from the masters and ustads of food their respective specialities, in their own environment. I have learned from pani-puri walas, cooks in dhabas, roadside vendors, food enthusiasts, YouTube videos, TV shows and chefs at fancy restaurants.

I've also learned a lot from just watching my own family cook. When the entire Hussain clan (the paternal side of my family) would meet at our ancestral home, Fazal Manzil, in Sasaram, Bihar, we would only talk about food. This tradition is still alive and, till date, when we meet in Delhi, our conversations rarely involve politics or other worldly problems. The most important topic is, and always has been, food.

Again, I'm lucky to have learned from the best. Ammi's love for food is on a completely different level. Her favourite phrase in the whole wide world is: '*Khana kha lo* (Eat food).' Even as we are finishing our lunch, she often asks us what we would like to eat for dinner. She learned how to cook from her own Ammi (my Nanna), who, in turn, is the grand chef of the family. I have found that it is simply impossible to go on a diet while staying with Ammi. She always serves the heaviest and creamiest food on the very day I plan to start a diet. Once, I remember telling her that I was planning to go on a low-carb diet for a week, but came home to find that she had made gajar ka halwa and biryani for dinner.

Surprised, I asked her why she had chosen that day (of all days) to make this food, suggesting I skip the meal. To this she scoffed and said, 'Start your diet tomorrow.' You see what I mean?

When you come from a family like mine, one is always surrounded by amazing delicacies, and it is very difficult to not want to talk about them all the time. Growing up, it quickly dawned on me that I wanted to do more than just talk about food; I wanted to be involved in the food industry. I never had the chance to actively pursue a culinary career, but I knew that it was my calling. When I moved to Delhi for work, I decided it was time to give my dream a shot. To give myself a break from the strain of my day job, I started a pop-up café called Bread and Better with my friend Manasi. We worked out of the kitchens of friends and family, and hosted friends and strangers alike for a pop-up meal once a month.

It was this entrepreneurial experience that gave me the confidence to audition for and later compete on MasterChef India in 2016. Cooking for three masters, chefs Kunal Kapur, Vikas Khanna and Zorawar Kalra, was no easy task. Each contestant had to put their best plate forward every day. We learned to cook in high-pressure environments, and to cope with this I put myself on a strict schedule to discipline myself. I'd get up at 5.30 a.m. to go for a run. I'd run 8 kilometres every day, from Bandra to Juhu Chowpatty, and spend some time alone on the beach, watching the waves. I would sit there for a while, listening to the birds, watching people run with their dogs and the garbage trucks make their rounds. Then, I'd head back to our hotel by 7.30 a.m. to get ready and leave for the shoot by 9 a.m., returning only at 9 or 10 p.m. The contestants would hang out together for a while, eating and chatting, and then we'd go to our rooms to learn more about dishes and plating styles, finally going to sleep by midnight. The intense experience that was MasterChef made me realize that I needed to take my love for food out of the kitchens and into the world. I wanted to make people fall in love with food, to feel the way I do when I cook.

I come from a culture with a rich culinary tradition, and I'm aware that it is impossible to do justice to the variety that is Indian Muslim food. There are many stories to tell from within it, revolving around meals. Growing up, Abbi told me that Muslims can eat anything as long as one is aware of the food being halal or haram. Islam divides food into three categories: halal (allowed), haram (prohibited) and *makruh* (strictly to be avoided as abominable). The traditional Muslim way of eating is very different, a *mukhtalif* (distinct) style. In a traditional Muslim household, food is always served on a yellow cloth placed neatly on the floor. This cloth is called a *dastarkhān,* which finds its origin in Persian. On this, food is served on big, shared platters. The dastarkhān is a meeting point, around which the whole family gathers to enjoy a meal. Once seated, someone comes around to help those seated wash their hands before and after dining.

Chitrita Banerji, in her book *Eating India,* writes: 'It is often easy to forget that the arrival of the Muslims was the first major external influence to radically reshape cooking and eating in India.'[1] Sultans, Shahs, Mughals, Nizams and Nawabs, all of these ruling dynasties changed the way Indians cooked their food. These periods saw the creation of dishes meant for royalty, commoners, labourers and warriors.

There is a popular quip that Muslims are 'pure non-vegetarians'. Now, I'm not saying this is entirely untrue, but bracketing them as a people that are fond of only non-vegetarian fare is only half the truth. It was a challenge to find vegetarian dishes to include in this book, and my research yielded not too many results, but a podcast by Shaykh Hamza Yusuf, an American-Islamic scholar, points out that meat is not a necessity in Shari'ah, and that in the old days, Muslims could only eat meat once a week, on Fridays, if they were wealthy, and only on Eid if they were poor.[2]

Another common misconception is that Muslim food consists of just biryani and kebabs. No doubt, these dishes are the brand ambassadors of Muslim cuisine, and one will most definitely be served at least one of these two dishes at a Muslim house, but there is a range of vegetarian and non-vegetarian dishes with complex backgrounds and interesting origins that most people know little of. In this book, there is no recipe for biryani since it is already well known. Instead, my aim is to broaden the horizon of what we know about Muslim cooking. The dishes I present, often, are similar to those eaten in non-Muslim households, but there are variations in the technique, and it is this nuance that I'd like to bring to your plate.

My love for history, research and storytelling led to the creation of my blog and, now, this book about food history and food stories. It is my pleasure to give you thirty stories and recipes of dishes from different families and cities that connect back to my own kitchen and experiences.

From my beautiful Bilqis Manzil and Fazal Manzil, to Ramgarh and Ranchi, and then the lanes of Khirki Extension in Delhi, my love for food has come a long way. I present to you *Daastan-e-Dastarkhān*, a tale of various tables. This book is an attempt to explore the unexplored and lesser-known dishes of families, restaurants and small eateries. These dishes are not necessarily 'Islamic', simply because food has no religion, but they do find their origin in kitchens which belonged to Muslim families of the yesteryears and till date continue to be found in many Muslim homes. I hope the stories presented offer a different facet of a cuisine that is far wider and richer than is popularly known.

# In the Beginning

# 1

# Aloo Salan

WHEN AMMI WAS A child, a pir baba would visit her house, Bilqis Manzil, on the first Thursday of every month during *zuhr* namaz, the afternoon prayer, to bless their home and family members. The saint was old and used a walking stick to support himself. He had a brown satchel, filled with religious books, slung over his shoulder, a leather pouch for water and some loose cash, which he'd collect from the houses he visited. His white, flowing robes and green turban made him seem taller and gaunter than he actually was. At every house, he'd recite *dua*s and hand out *misri* (sugar candy), which he had blessed, to kids to protect them against the evil eye. After namaz, he'd spend time with the children narrating verses from the Quran and finally, return to the mosque after *asr* namaz (the evening prayer).

It is said that once you receive *dua*s from pir fakirs, you should never send them away without offering alms and food. And so, every time the pir baba visited their home, my Nanna would cook for him. Ammi and the other kids would lay out the yellow dastarkhān on the verandah and serve lunch, which would usually be aloo gosht stuffed with melt-in-the-mouth meat pieces, steamed rice, cucumber and onion salad, achaar (pickle) and lukewarm water.

One day, the pir baba visited Bilqis Manzil on a Wednesday instead of the usual Thursday. My Nanna panicked because there was no meat at home. She wracked her brain for an alternate recipe. She quickly rustled up a salan using a dried fig and posto (poppy seed) paste, tossed in some fried potatos, while balancing the flavours with garam masala and chillies. She served this dish with steamed rice and besan ki roti on their dastarkhān.

When the pir baba ate the dish, he became a *mureed* (fan) of my Nanna's food all over again and blessed her with long life saying, 'Allah *kare aapke ghar me khana kabhi kam na ho aur aapke ghar se koi bhookha kabhi na jaye* (May Allah bless you with an abundance of food and may no one ever leave your home hungry).'

The same pir baba gave Abbi a *taviz* when he had lost his job and was struggling in life. Soon after wearing the *taviz* and following the pir baba's instructions, Abbi got a job and became financially stable. The pir baba died a few years ago, but his blessings still nourish our family. We always have food in our kitchen, and perhaps it is because of his very blessings that my younger cousin, Shaghil, and I have both pursued a culinary profession.

A salan is essentially just a spiced curry and one can come up with many variations depending on what you use as the primary ingredient. Aloo salan is one of the easiest comfort foods that Ammi has in her repertoire of recipes. Whenever she doesn't have enough time to cook or is feeling lazy, this is what she makes. In fact, this dish regularly features in both my maternal and paternal family's meals. We usually club it with steamed rice or plain roti. And, of course, aloo salan is popular because of its main ingredient – the potato.

During Lalu Yadav's political reign in Bihar one would often hear this saying, '*Jab tak rahega* samosa *mein aloo, tab tak rahega*

Bihar *mein* Lalu (As long as there is potato stuffing in a samosa, there will be Lalu Yadav in Bihar).' Tell any Indian that their beloved potato came to India only a few hundred years ago, and they'll look at you in disbelief and ask you to stop telling lies. But nothing can be truer than the potato's foreign origins.

In *History of Agriculture in India up to C.1200* AD, it is recorded that, 'Early domesticated potatoes were found in central Peru which has been dated R-14 to 7000 BCE. It is likely that the potato might have been domesticated in the Lake Titicaca to Lake Poopó region of north Bolivia. Potato was originally known as "camata" or "batata" in the Caribbean and travelled to Spain and other parts of Europe in the sixteenth century. "Batata" became "potato" when it went to England.'[3] In Maharashtra, this spud continues to be called 'batata'.

Further, Bibhu Prasad Singh and Rajesh K. Rana in their paper 'History of Potato and its Emerging Problems in India' state that it was the Portuguese who, in the early seventeenth century, introduced the potato to India.[4] The British took the potato to the hills in northern India and Sri Lanka, where it prospered as an important plant in the gardens of colonial homes. Historical evidence suggests that the potato was a well-established garden crop in Surat and Karnataka as early as 1675, while potato cultivation was introduced in Shimla in 1828 and the Nilgiri Hills in 1830.

According to Dr K.T. Achaya in *A Historical Dictionary of Indian Food,* Europeans in India were the first to introduce potatoes in kitchens, followed by the Muslims. But it was the Dutch who popularized the potato. When the potato first made its appearance in markets, it was viewed with suspicion and there was wild speculation about how it was bad for one's health and that it increased people's sex drive.[5] We've come a long way from those days. According to a report published in 2017 by Jessica

Lynn, India is the second-largest producer of potatoes in the world, producing 45.34 million metric tons of potatoes per year.[6] Let's just say the potato is here to stay and flourish.

Aloo is a chameleon vegetable that goes well with every dish, be it meat, vegetables or rice. It is one of the most basic ingredients of north Indian cuisine. When cooked properly with curry and meat, aloo tends to absorb the flavour of both the meat and the spices, taking on a new character with every dish. Cheap, readily available and versatile, potatoes have given us many delicious dishes. From chokha, to the stuffing of pani puri, the masala of a dosa, chaat, and, of course, aloo ke parathe, the sheer variety of potato dishes is unmatched. But the simple dish of aloo salan is one of my favourites.

Since Ammi couldn't remember how Nanna made the dish with fig, I turned to the primary source. As I mentioned previously, Nanna is the grand chef of our family. She is a traditionalist who avoids technology as much as possible (except to watch my YouTube videos, which she enjoys critiquing). She never uses a mixer or a grinder to grind spices, still preferring the traditional *sil-batta* to make chutnies and pastes, and whenever possible, using earthen pots to cook.

This aloo salan recipe is generations old, but with my Nanna's special twist. Since it's from Nanna's memory, which is commendable, I know that this was exactly what was served to the pir baba so many years ago, before I was born. Nanna never used recipe books or wrote down instructions anywhere. For her, cooking is part of her muscle memory. She practices her dishes over and over again to perfect their flavour and texture. Personally, I don't think this dish needs a fixed recipe because I believe every family has their own version – made with their own spices, varying the thickness of the salan depending on their taste. This simple, hearty and nourishing dish precedes me; I think of it as Ammi's and Abbi's, and also the pir baba's, the one who blessed our family. In a way, Nanna's simple offering of potatoes and meat is my origin story, because this is where my culinary journey began.

---

## Recipe

Serves: 4
Cooking time: 40 minutes

### Ingredients

- 2 tbsp mustard oil
- 1 large onion, chopped
- 1 tsp cumin seeds
- ½ tsp fresh ginger, crushed
- 1 tsp fresh garlic, crushed
- 4 tomatoes, chopped
- 1 small green chilli, chopped
- 1 tsp coriander powder
- 2 tsp posto dana paste (poppy seeds)
- 1 tsp black pepper, crushed
- 1 tsp turmeric powder
- 1 tsp cumin powder
- ½ tsp chilli powder
- Salt to taste
- 12 small potatoes, boiled and fried whole
- 2 dried figs, diced
- Water
- Fresh coriander leaves to garnish

## Method

1. In a medium-sized saucepan, heat the mustard oil till it start to smoke.
2. Add the chopped onion and sauté until it turns translucent.
3. Add the cumin seeds and let it splutter, then add the ginger and garlic. Cook for 3–4 minutes before adding the tomatoes, green chilli and all the spices with salt.
4. Add the potatoes and mix well with all the spices.
5. Toss in the posto paste, diced figs, add water and bring to a boil.
6. Reduce the heat, and let it simmer for 10–12 minutes.
7. Adjust the gravy's consistency as per your taste.
8. Garnish with coriander and serve.

# 2

# Kairi aur Kathal Dopiaza

EVERY MAY, WHEN THE sun turns the earth as dry and flaky as a puff pastry and our school closed for two months, Ammi would begin preparations for our summer holiday. For as long as I can remember, it had been our family's tradition to spend this break with my grandparents in Sasaram, Bihar. Sasaram is an ancient city and finds early mentions during the Vedic period. This city has witnessed the legacy of Sahastrabahu, Sher Shah Suri and Jagjivan Ram Babu, and served as a gateway to the Nalanda and Gaya area.

While Ammi would wrap up the house work, pack our things and get ready for the trip, I'd find the old rhyme, '*Nani ghar jayenge, doodh malai khayenge, mote hoke aayenge* (Going to my grandmother's house to eat milk cream and come back fat),' playing on my lips. But I must clarify here that I was already a fat, round kid, and very proud to be one, in fact. Most children dream of becoming pilots, engineers, doctors or managers, but I was different; I wanted to be the fattest kid in the world! I don't know how I came to nurture this noble goal, but I actively pursued it till I was about 12 years old. And one of the most effective ways to realize my dream was spending summers at Sasaram because the food at my grandparents' house was unparalleled.

On the morning of our departure, Ammi would dress us in comfortable clothes, and dragging our bags, we'd stand outside our house in Ramgarh, which was on the national highway, and wait for the 8.30 a.m. bus. The eight-hour journey would fly by with us eating bags of peanuts and chips, drinking cups of tea and interacting with the many vendors selling snacks or toys at every stop. But the highlight of the trip was the home-cooked food Ammi always packed. I forever associate the spread of puri, aloo or parwal ki sabzi (preparation of potato or pointed gourd) and achaar with travel, because no matter where I went as a child, and even later, I'd eat this dish en route. Later, when I journeyed extensively across north India, I realized this humble spread was, in fact, universally considered travel food in the region.

There were many similarities between my paternal and maternal grandparents. They both lived in the same neighbourhood, Nooran Ganj, they had similar sprawling bungalows, which like twins had (almost) identical names – Bilqis Manzil and Fazal Manzil. We would usually stay at Bilqis Manzil, my Nanna's house, which had 15 rooms, including two kitchens and four storerooms, and a huge *aangan* (courtyard). This courtyard was the social epicentre of the house. In it, there was a henna tree that always came to the rescue of the ladies of the family during Eid. They'd pluck the fresh leaves, grind them into a paste and use this to decorate their hands. Bilqis Manzil was home to three parrots, who my Nanna would fuss over, feeding them fruit and chillies. It was also home to a few chickens and roosters, who were always loitering around, and would give us fresh eggs every morning. In the backyard, there was a flourishing garden with orange and palm trees and three guava trees. I'd climb the guava trees, racing against the squirrels to get to the sweetest fruit first. My favourite spot was the wooden swing under the trees, the hangout place for the family's younger folk. As a child I would have my breakfast and my milk on the swing. Even though it was my Bade Mamu (uncle) who had laid the garden's foundations, it was Chote Mamu, my youngest uncle, who lovingly tended to it.

On reaching my grandparent's home, the first thing I'd do was hog on the soft, melt-in-your-mouth chocolates that Majhle Mamu would bring from Saudi Arabia. In the evenings, my first stop in Sasaram would always be 'Aunty's shop' located on a footpath outside the Nooran Ganj mosque. Here, in the evenings, you'd find groups of elderly people catching up on gossip and news over cups of hot tea, while the younger children boisterously rode their bicycles and played *lattu* (wooden top). If the weather was right, we'd bring out our kites to fly or play cricket. Aunty's shop sold candy, biscuits, local chips and other snacks, but the thing that drew me to her was her 'aloo cut' – boiled potatoes, sliced and dipped in tangy tamarind water and sprinkled with her secret spice mix. Served in a leaf bowl and costing just ₹3, it was a delicious snack that I couldn't get enough of. '*Arre beta, aa gaye tum* (Son, you have come back)?' Aunty would say to me warmly, even though I barely knew her, and so I'd return her kindness by wolfing down at least two plates of her wonderful offering.

I'd spend those languorous summer mornings in lazy inertia, watching TV shows like *Aladdin, Captain Vyom* and *Boogie Woogie,* sauntering around the cool house while eating biju mangoes – a tiny variety that can only be sucked on, rather than being sliced, and which, unfortunately, isn't easily found these days. Mangoes were a sweet upside to the oppressive heat, and they were another reason I loved going to Sasaram. Timed perfectly with our holiday, many different varieties of mangoes would arrive from our farms in Ara, Bihar, my favourites being the juicy malda and langda varieties.

On one such morning I found Baby Aunty, our house help at Nanna's, peeling raw biju mangoes. Curious, I asked her what she was planning to do with them. Was she going to pickle them? Her answer surprised me. She told me she was going to cook the mangoes with kathal (jackfruit). I was puzzled. Why cook something which could be consumed just by itself?

Even though I love jackfruit in all its forms – ripe, pickled, cooked in gravy, or even just the roasted seeds of a ripe jackfruit as a snack – I can understand why many people don't feel the same way about this fruit. When ripe, its slippery texture, distinct fragrance and sweet taste make it somewhat of an acquired taste. The first Mughal emperor belonged to this camp. 'Babur liked mangoes and bananas but compared jackfruit to the "revolting intestines of a sheep",' writes Annemarie Schimmel in her book, *The Empire of the Great Mughals: History, Art and Culture.*[7] Some people say that the texture of jackfruit is the same as lamb meat, but I disagree. I think the jackfruit's flavour and texture are unmatched and I love how versatile it is in its usage. As a fan of the fruit, it was interesting to find this little story about jackfruit in Devdutt Pattanaik's book, *Jaya: An Illustrated Retelling of the Mahabharata*. The story goes that one day, Bhima, who was being playful, lay in bed and pretended to be running a high fever. He had slipped two jackfruits under the sheet and then requested Draupadi to massage his feet. Draupadi, unaware of the deception, massaged the fruit thinking they were Bhima's feet. Bhima burst out laughing at the sight of Draupadi getting tricked. When the truth was later revealed to Draupadi, she became angry and cursed the fruit that its smooth jacket would forever be covered in spikes.[8]

But back to Baby Aunty. According to her, kathal dopiaza was the perfect summer dish, because firstly, mangoes were in season, and secondly, raw mango added the right kind of tartness to the dish. With 18 to 20 people to cook for and only a few hours to lunch, Baby Aunty didn't have the time to answer my many questions, so I set about observing first-hand the making of this dish.

She began by sautéing the onion and ginger–garlic paste till the onions were nicely browned and caramelized. Then she tossed in a couple of spices and added the chopped kathal, leaving it to cook for a few minutes. In the end, she tossed in the sliced mangoes, fried onions and then cooked the dish on a very low flame for about 20 minutes. When it was almost done, she threw in some dried apricots to balance the tartness.

I didn't know it then, but the technique Baby Aunty was using to pull together the mango and jackfruit is a Mughlai style of cooking called 'dopiaza'. The word literally means 'two onions' in Persian. All of us are familiar with some form of dopiaza, and the technique itself is pretty straightforward: in the method, onions are used at two different stages, in two different ways – the onion paste and the caramelized onion, both of which impart a distinct texture to the dish.

But it is the dopiaza's origin story that is my favourite. Part of popular lore, it goes something like this. A long time ago in Agra, a schoolmaster's son, Abdul Hasan, had a big dream; he longed to be a part of Emperor Akbar's famous court. His dream was realized when he became chief of the royal poultry farm. Abdul Hasan worked hard and proved his worth by considerably bringing down the operational costs of the farm. This brought him to the king's notice, and he was soon promoted to chief librarian, where, once again, he proved his extraordinary skills. This time Akbar promoted him further, making him one of the Navratnas, or nine gems in his court – an honour that Abdul Hasan had always wanted.

What made me love Abdul Hasan was his love for food, and so I began to look for more stories about him. This led me to an online repository of food stories called 'Kitchens of History', which credits him for creating the dopiaza technique.[9] Just the way my love for food led me to Abdul Hasan, his led him to a book of recipes from the Kingdom of Mandu called the *Nimmatnama-i Nasiruddin-Shahi.*[10] (This book is in fact in the Jawaharlal Nehru University Library in New Delhi. The book has an English translation and some real hand-painted pictures of the Mughal court, scriptures, vessels and pots.)

Abdul Hasan was a true gourmand, and would often throw many lavish parties at his home, with one of the prime objectives being to test his cooking. At one such event, Hasan was trying out a recipe from the *Nimmatnama-i Nasiruddin-Shahi*, and found the instructions frustratingly confusing. After much trial and error, he realized the benefit of adding onions to the dish, at different points, and instructed his kitchen staff to add it every time he clapped. The dish came out wonderfully, and when Akbar finally tried it, he loved it and asked for it repeatedly. This might be how Abdul Hasan came to be known as Mullah Dopiaza.

That day, many years ago, Baby Aunty served us kairi (unripe mango) aur kathal dopiaza with steamed rice and a tangy raw mango pickle. Even though she didn't know the story behind how the dopiaza method came to be, she was familiar with the technique that gave the dish its distinct flavour. These days, restaurants add tomatoes to the gravy to increase its body and thickness as a shortcut. But wouldn't it be a shame if Mullah Dopiaza's story was lost forever? Food is as much about eating and community as it is about its stories. These small food stories are important and should be passed down generations to ensure the survival of both the dish and their narratives.

I was only 13 years old then, and I was just beginning to scrape the surface of the treasure trove of stories that hid beneath the flavours of food. But there was something in me that pushed me down this trail. Today, when I serve my family versions of dopiaza for lunch, I tell them Mullah Dopiaza's story and it always delights them. In fact, because of this, Shaghil wanted to learn the whole process from start to finish, and soon, we were in the kitchen, our aprons on, cooking away.

---

## Recipe

Serves: 4
Cooking time: 40 to 45 minutes

### Ingredients

- ¼ cup oil
- ½ kg kathal (jackfruit), cut into small pieces
- ¼ cup ghee
- 1 tbsp cumin seeds
- 1 bay leaf
- 4 whole peppercorns
- 4 cloves
- 3 dried red chillies
- ½ tsp powdered fenugreek
- 1 tsp powdered fennel seeds
- 1 cup onion, grated
- 1 tsp ginger paste
- 1 tsp garlic paste
- ½ cup yoghurt
- 1 small kairi (raw mango), diced
- 1 tsp garam masala
- Salt to taste

- ½ tsp turmeric
- 1 tbsp coriander powder
- 1 tsp chilli powder
- 2 dried apricots, diced
- 2 green chillies, slit
- 2 cups fried onions
- Fresh coriander to garnish

## Method

1. Heat oil in a deep pan and fry the kathal pieces till they turn golden brown.
2. In another deep pan, heat ghee and add the cumin seeds, bay leaf, peppercorns, cloves, dried red chillies, powdered fenugreek and fennel seeds till it splutters.
3. Add onion and ginger–garlic paste. Cook over a medium flame till the rawness disappears and the paste turns brown.
4. Toss in all the fried pieces of kathal and ensure that it is mixed well with the masala. Maintain the medium heat.
5. Beat the yoghurt and mix it into the pan with the kathal, ensuring that the flame is on low. Stir vigorously to blend the yoghurt with the paste and kathal.
6. Add the diced mangoes and increase the flame to medium. Cook till the oil separates.
7. Add the garam masala, salt, turmeric, coriander, chilli powder and dried apricot.
8. Mix well, then add fresh green chillies and fried onions.
9. Continue cooking over medium heat for five more minutes and then take it off the flame.
10. Garnish with chopped coriander and serve hot with rotis or steamed rice.

# 3

# Ratalu Kachalu ki Chaat

AT AROUND 2 P.M., Raju Bhai, our local chaat vendor in Sasaram, would assemble his many pots, pans and ingredients on his *thela* (cart) and set off for the day. His destination was the government school in Chowkhandi, 2 kilometres from Bilqis and Fazal Manzil, where he would sell his wares all evening. As he made his way there, a distance covered in ten or fifteen minutes, Raju Bhai would gain a trail of followers stopping him every step of the way for a plate of his chaat and pani puri. This had been going on for many years, and Raju Bhai had his loyal base of customers for whom he'd tailor the flavours according to their preferences. Even Ammi loved his chaat and used to have it all the time when she was young. She'd tell me that the only thing that had changed about Raju Bhai's chaat was that it used to cost just fifty paisa back then.

The very word 'chaat' was enough to make my mouth water. At once sweet, salty, tangy, crispy, velvety, hot, cold – chaat is an explosion of flavours and textures, enough to totally confuse your palate. 'Chaat' means to lick, which comes from the fact that the spices linger on your tastebuds, prompting you to literally lick your fingers (or at times the plate as well!) when you're done. The most important ingredient in chaat is the masala – a delectable amalgamation of amchoor (mango powder), kala namak (rock salt), cumin, dried ginger, coriander, black pepper, red chilli and salt.

Raju Bhai's chaat was an elaborate preparation which included fried aloo tikkis, spices, whisked curd, chutney, and all of this for just ₹5. Even after many years, when I went back to Sasaram, I saw that Raju Bhai's chaat was still selling like hot cakes; two generations have since joined the business, adding more helping hands, which allowed him to serve more customers. But the one thing that has remained unchanged is the flavour and honesty in his food.

Chaat, in a way, is a great way to use leftovers. In our house in Ramgarh, Ammi would make a samosa chaat on Sunday evenings in which she would basically make use of the leftover chole from our breakfast. She would buy fresh samosas, mash them on a plate, top it up with the chole, add imli (tamarind) and coriander chutney, along with curd, freshly chopped onions, black salt and chaat masala. Surprisingly, the flavour profile would change drastically. For the longest time Ammi tricked us with this jugaad, but once I grew up and started watching my weight, I cut down on the amount of chole and samose I would have in the mornings and eventually Ammi also started making less of it.

But that was much later. As a child, I loved chaat. And often, on Sundays, Abbi would take my elder brother, Shabi, and me on his green Bajaj Chetak scooter to the main vegetable market. He'd either treat us to chole bhature outside the vegetable market or chaat opposite Priya Sweet House. There were three chaat carts. One of the vendors reminded me of Raju Bhai because he'd welcome us with a big smile and customize the chaat according to our preference. After our chaat stop, we'd go to Gift House to buy Big Babol, Center Fresh or Boomer chewing gum and collect the free cricket cards that came with them. The joys of childhood!

It was in Ramgarh that another chaat wala, Babloo Bhaiya, taught me a nifty technique to chop onions. He would use a thin, sharp blade and chop the whole onion in his hand in a freestyle method. No boards, no base, and definitely no easy feat. Every evening, Babloo Bhaiya would pass by my house shooting me a smile. It was his way of checking whether I wanted chaat and pani puri or not.

From the regular bhalla aloo chaat to raj kachori to shahi bhalla chaat, the variations of chaat around the country is mind-boggling. Every part of India has its own version of chaat. In Agra and Rajasthan, I've eaten shahi bhalla and found it really interesting; the masalas and ingredients are the same, but the surprise element is when you cut the bhalla open and dry fruit bursts out. The dry fruit not only add a crunchy texture but also a sweet flavour. Then there's the Bhaukaal chaat in Varanasi near Assi Ghat. The word *bhaukaal* means 'boasting' or 'showing off', and is a common term in Lucknow. To be honest I didn't quite like the chaat, but the preparation, with freshly cut tomatoes and finely chopped onions on top, was fascinating. I liked talking to the Bhaukaal chaat vendor about his food and Assi Ghat more than eating his chaat.

It's only when I moved to Delhi many years later that I would realize the city's unparalleled love for chaat and pani puri, and how loyal Dilliwalas are to their own chaat bhaiyas. Old Delhi is a paradise for chaat lovers. One of the oldest and most famous chaat shop is Natraj Dahi Bhalle Wala (opposite Paranthe Wali Gali). It's so small and unremarkable, you'll probably miss it at first glance, but their chaat is a lip-smacking experience. While I was waiting in line once, I got into conversation with some other customers who seemed to be loving their aloo tikki. They told me that the chaat here has a traditional flavour, and that it is unique and couldn't be found anywhere else in Delhi. I ordered a plate of dahi bhalle which, indeed, was out of this world. It was a romance of spices on my palate – garnished with a perfectly spiced chutney, saunth (dried ginger), ginger and a secret masala.

Deep in the alleys of Chawri Bazaar, there's the 200-year-old Kulle ki Chaat, a popular shop that serves a unique fruit chaat. The vendor scoops out the pulp from a fruit to make a cavity in the centre and then fills the shell with boiled chickpeas and pomegranate, mixing them with different spices, chaat masala, sugar and lemon juice. Each bite gives you a different taste because of the many fruits and vegetables used.

But where did chaat come from?

There is no single authoritative story about the origins of chaat. Some say it comes from Bengal, others from Delhi, while there are those who claim it comes from outside India. Let's not even begin to debate which state has the best chaat because no two people will agree. However, there is a popular story about chaat's origins that I particularly like. It is believed that the credit goes to the royal hakim (doctor) and khansamas of the great Emperor Shah Jahan in Delhi. When the emperor built his empire in Delhi, his *shahi* (chief) hakim was enraged. He told the emperor that the water in the Yamuna was not favourable for cooking and if people ate food cooked in that water, they would fall sick and die. Shah Jahan couldn't relocate again, so he asked the hakim to offer him a solution. The shahi hakim suggested that spicy food, containing fat, would help sustain people. Spicy food helps retain body heat and fat helps cool one down and reduces the damage done by the spices. Hence, chaat came to be, in the walled city of Dilli. Today chaat has been adapted into our modern culinary techniques, and it has also found its way into fine-dining menus across the seas to become popular internationally.

While most of us cannot imagine chaat without potato, it can be made with other roots and yams. Ratalu (yam) and kachalu (cocoyam) are two examples of how Indians enjoy the roots of vegetables. This recipe is an attempt to get back to our roots and recreate the flavour of these chaats of yore.

Making chaat is not difficult or tricky, but it does demand a control on the quantity of spices, chutney and yoghurt used, so that each complements the other. Too much or too little of these elements will ruin the dish. Balance is key. In fact, when Babloo Bhai would make chaat, he'd always take our feedback and ask whether the flavour worked for us. Did we need more salt, tartness or anything else? It is the balance of flavours and textures in a humble plate of chaat that makes it special. I sometimes wonder about the number of trials that must have happened to make the first flavourful plate of chaat, and what the royals must have said to the khansamas.

---

## Recipe

Serves: 2
Cooking time: 35 to 40 minutes

### Ingredients

- 1 medium ratalu (yam), roasted
- 3 small kachalu (arbi), roasted
- 4 tbsp ghee
- 1½ tbsp imli (tamarind) chutney
- 1½ tbsp green chutney (see Appendix)

- 1 tsp red chilli powder
- 1 tsp chaat masala
- 1 tsp roasted cumin (jeera) powder
- 1–2 green chillies, finely chopped
- 1 tbsp lemon juice
- 1 tbsp chopped coriander leaves
- 8–10 fried cashew nuts and raisins (optional)
- Pomegranate seeds and star fruit for garnish

## Method

1. Peel and dice the roasted ratalu and kachalu.
2. In a pan, heat the ghee and fry the kachalu till they are golden brown.
3. In another bowl mix all the spices and chutnies with the roasted ratalu and the pan-fried kachalu. Mix in the green chillies, coriander leaves and lemon juice.
4. Top it with dry fruit, and garnish with pomegranate and slices of star fruit.

# 4

# Nanna ke Mughlai Parathe

EVERYONE IN MY FAMILY has many stories to tell about Nanna, my maternal grandmother, and almost all of them have food at its heart. They say that even a simple roti made by her tasted amazing. They were thinner and softer than any other roti they'd ever had. So when it came to matters related to food, everyone would seek her expert advice.

During Ramzan, Nanna could always be found on the verandah of Bilqis Manzil (the house was named after her), chopping fruit and vegetables for a salad, while others hovered around her to get a final approval on the other dishes. I remember the month of Ramzan with great fondness as it was a time the entire family would come together to celebrate the festival of Eid. It was a time to share, celebrate and bond.

Our days during Ramzan would pan out something like this. The adults in the family *rozedar* (people who are observing the fast) would wake up at 3 a.m. for *sehri,* the meal that is eaten before sunrise, while the children only managed to stir 10 minutes before *sehri* was over, just in the nick of time to quickly shovel down some food before going back to sleep. In our family the tradition was to eat light, fulfilling food in the morning. So, the menu usually comprised of dalia (a porridge), sevai (vermicelli) and other light food – a balanced mix with enough sugar, carbohydrate and fibre to get through the day. Nanna and the other elders of the family would go for their *fajr* namaz (morning prayer) while Chote Mamu would switch on the water pump to fill the main tank and the buckets, and only then would he pray. He'd then clean his bike, which he was very fond of, and then get ready to head to court around 8 in the morning. The rest of the family would spend the day reading the Quran, sleeping, cooking for the kids, while the children played Ludo. I'd be the first one to bring out the board and entice my cousins to a game. My favourite colour was blue and so it was always my first choice of buttons, unless the younger ones complained. We had a saying: 'Blue *bulata hai, hara harata hai, lal lalchata hai aur pila pilata hai* (Blue calls the other pieces to it, green will defeat you, red will simply tease you, and yellow is useless).'

As the day wound down, and the time of iftar, or the evening meal, drew near, everyone would once again gather in our big *aangan*, the beautiful space full of green plants and a small henna tree in the corner, to lay down the dastarkhān. It was the younger lot's duty to help set it up under the watchful eyes of Chote Mamu and Majhle Mamu. Our dastarkhān would be laid out with sherbet, dates, two kinds of pakora with green chutney and tomato ketchup, channa ghugni, fruit salad, steamed rice, kebabs, or pan-tossed meat, and something sweet like moongechi, jalebi or meethe samose. While the elders cooked and served the food and the children bustled around doing smaller errands, Nanna would be at the centre of this storm, encouraging, giving instructions and scolding us if she saw something being done incorrectly. She was the authority figure, the driver of this chaotic, but well-oiled machine. She'd also take the iftar food out for *mohtaj* (dependants) and send three or four portions to the mosque near our house.

Once everything was served and laid out, and the azan from the nearby mosque sang into the evening, we would sit down and feast. We would talk and make fun of the younger children and boss them around, but usually because we would be so hungry, our conversations were limited to asking others to pass on the bowl of fruit, pakora, ghugni water and other delicacies that were served. Post iftar, the funniest and the most satisfying part of the discussion would ensue: we'd start discussing what we would eat for dinner while sipping on our evening tea! The food wasn't even digested in our tummies and we'd be talking about what to eat next!

After eating, the men and boys of the family would make their way to the mosque to pray, and the ladies would settle in the big room adjoining the *aangan* to offer namaz. Once completed, the feast resumed. This time, it was dinner. Unlike iftar, dinner was never eaten at the same table or at the same time – it would depend on people's moods and how hungry they were. The table would be laid and remain spread till midnight, and sometimes all night long, till we woke up for *sehri*. Dinner usually consisted of non-vegetarian dishes to provide protein and balance our meal, helping us recover from the whole day of fasting. It also included the leftovers from iftar.

My favourite pastime during Ramzan, when not playing Ludo, was to hang around in the kitchen with my lalla (my mother's youngest sister) and mami (my mother's brother's wife), learning their tricks and techniques. The kitchen was the only place that was always busy and buzzing and so I preferred being in there more than anywhere else. It was here that the foundation blocks of my love for cooking were laid. As I grew up, I effortlessly transitioned from an eager audience to a willing participant.

Last Ramzan, I was in Ghaziabad (where my extended family now resides), which often turns into a mini-Sasaram. The dishes on the menu were similar to what I used to eat as a child. Inspired after watching one of my YouTube videos, my mami decided to make luqmi – a square, fried pastry with a meat stuffing. Luqmi comes from the Urdu word *luqma*, which means 'bite-sized'. It is essentially a bite-sized meat samosa. As I was rolling out the dough, Nanna came and sat next to me. Being a fantastic cook herself, she's always been interested in my life as a chef and loves to hear about my experiences. She asked me if I had ever eaten a Mughlai paratha. I nodded yes, imagining the one I had eaten at a Durga Puja pandal in Delhi. A Mughlai paratha is basically a crispy, deep-fried, stuffed meat paratha made of thinly rolled maida (white flour); this is served with green chutney and butter. Nanna laughed and told me that whatever I had eaten wasn't a Mughlai paratha but a close imitation.

She explained that '*parat*' means layer and '*atta*' means flour, and when you combine these two words or elements you get a 'paratha'. A real Mughlai paratha (or as the Bengalis call it, Moghlai porotha) must have extremely soft dough that is rolled thin enough to look like translucent paper, to which ghee is then applied. This dough is collected back, folded and rolled out again a few more times. The secret to a good Mughlai paratha lies in the technique of folding the dough and frying it at the perfect temperature – shallow fried on a low flame to make sure it's cooked through and retains its crispiness. My lalla gave me another trade secret – the dough should be so light that it floats on water. Nanna also gave me many ideas for what the stuffing could be – her personal favourite is eggs topped with some soaked nuts. My time spent with my nani and dadi or anyone from the older generation has been priceless because they have so many interesting insights and secrets to share.

I learned about the history of the Mughlai paratha from an article in *The Hindu* written by Sumit Paul.[11] The story goes that Emperor Jahangir was bored of eating simple parathas with keema and so he challenged his cook, Adil Hafiz Usman, to come up with a recipe that was unique and unconventional. Usman came up with zabir-fala, or anda-roti, which later gained popularity as Mughlai parathas. Jahangir was delighted and rewarded him richly. To protect the source of his richness, Usman passed on the hit recipe to his son Farogh, who then shared it with his own sons, but made them swear to share it no further, thus creating the exclusivity of the dish.

However, Kalyan Karmakar, author of *The Travelling Belly*, writes in his blog that the dish isn't 'Mughlai' at all. In an interview with his friend, Prita, he asks whether this dish truly is 'Mughal' and she admits that calling the parathas 'Mughlai' was more of a branding exercise to grab the attention of customers. She points out that these parathas are not offered in traditional Muslim-run eateries. At most one can find rolls, but not Mughlai parathas.[12]

There will never be one exact story about the origin of a dish unless it is documented at its birth. But it is precisely this, the contradictory and sometimes downright unbelievable alternative narratives, that make food stories all the more interesting and magical. In a way, this book is my attempt to freeze and capture the tales about my family, especially those about Nanna. And so the recipe I'm putting down here is Nanna's. It is a dedication to her undying curiosity for food and her single-minded determination to serve only the most delicious fare.

Now that we have all grown up, we rarely go to Sasaram during Ramzan or otherwise. Chote Mamu, Mami and their children have moved out of Bilqis Manzil. Nanna has grown old and doesn't move around much. She lives with my other mamu and aunt in Ghaziabad. We have all fallen prey to the vagaries of time. But every Ramzan, as I eat or cook my first iftar, I am always transported to those golden years in Bilqis Manzil, when our humble dastarkhān brought us all together for a moment in time.

---

## Recipe

Serves: 3 to 4

Cooking time: 120 minutes

### Ingredients

- 2 tbsp ghee
- 2 cups water (for the dough)
- 3 cups flour
- 4 eggs
- 4 tbsp cooked keema (minced meat)
- ½ cup onion, finely chopped
- Salt to taste
- 2 green chillies, chopped
- 4 tbsp coriander leaves, chopped
- Oil for frying
- Chopped and fried dry fruits (almonds and cashews)

### Method

1. Mix the ghee, water and flour together and knead till a soft dough emerges. Cover it with a damp cloth. Leave it aside for 60–90 minutes.
2. Break the eggs in a bowl, and mix in the keema, onion, salt, green chillies, freshly chopped coriander leaves and dry fruit.

3. Divide the dough into five round balls, cover and leave it to rest for about 10 minutes.
4. Roll out the dough to make a flat, rectangular shaped roti.
5. Put 3–4 tbsp of the mixture in the middle.
6. Seal the ends by folding over four ways towards the centre, so that the ends overlap, forming a square.
7. Fry it on each side till it turns golden-brown.
8. Serve hot with either chutney or yoghurt, or both.

# 5

# Bihari Kebab

EID WAS A LITERAL food festival at Bilqis Manzil, but to ensure that everything went smoothly everyone was assigned a task. After the *qurbani* (sacrifice) of the animal, Chote Mamu would make sure that the meat came back neatly packed to our house; we usually got our meat on the first day after *qurbani*. Since the *aangan* was usually the venue for cooking on bigger occasions, Chote Mamu would supervise its cleaning or do it himself.

Then, Nanna would take over, sorting the meat into portions that would be given away to *mohtaj*, assigning different cuts for the biryani, kebab, nihari, keema and other dishes that would be made. In front of her, there would be different bowls for different cuts – boneless meat to mince for keema, boneless meat from the rear legs for kebab (my favourite) because it is soft, delicious and has the perfect amount of fat for kebabs. Ammi would always reserve the shank or tenderloin for boti kebabs and the ribs for pan-fried mutton kebabs. A woodfire would be lit and in no time the smells of cooking would fill the house.

In Ramgarh, we would cook kebabs differently. Ammi would put a slab on the floor to light the charcoal and use four bricks to rest the skewed meat, cooking it over a slow flame. Recently, on her birthday, I got her an electric grill, which did away with the cumbersome set-up and the use of charcoal. Because of this grill, we now eat Bihari kebabs often. Although, Ammi has discovered another way of cooking the same kebabs by using a pan. This tawa kebab has a unique flavour, especially when cooked with curry leaves.

As you can see, kebabs are beloved in our family. During Eid-ul-Zuha (Bakrid), if there are no kebabs on the menu, it's like we didn't celebrate the festival at all. As a child, Eid didn't come around in the summer, and I remember the simple delight of sitting by the woodfire, watching kebabs being cooked or how the *khur* (feet) of the animal were boiled for nihari for the next day's breakfast.

There's no snack quite as fulfilling and delicious as a well-made kebab. And the first step to making a good Bihari kebab is to thinly slice the meat, so that when it is marinated the flavours are absorbed thoroughly, the meat pieces stick together properly, and it cooks easily. When the meat is marinated with an assortment of spices, the end result is a kebab that simply melts in your mouth. From sumac, ghora, garam masala, onion, garlic and curd, there are innumerable marinades used in kebab-making across the world. But the ones I had as a child had something special about them. They were spicier. Once marinated for eight to 10 hours, the meat would be ready to be cooked. Lalla, Mami and Ammi would sit together, one of them would put the meat on the skewers, and the others would cook them on the open fire, basting them with ghee at regular intervals. According to Ammi, it is important to baste the meat with ghee while roasting so as to keep the kebab tender and moist on the inside, and this also imparts a rich flavour. Today, however, people prefer butter over ghee, which has its upside as it gives the meat a luxurious salty flavour.

Kebabs have been an integral part of my life. It is one of those dishes that can lift my mood instantly. Growing up, my favourite treat was the Bihari kebab. They are bigger pieces and also spicier, unlike other versions in the country. It also holds a special place in kebab legacy and hierarchy for me because I grew up enjoying these succulent and spicy offerings. Bisma Tirmizi, author of *Feast with a Taste of Amir Khusro*, shares her recipe of Bihari kebabs in *Dawn*, and it is exactly the way my family makes it. The recipe calls for sattu (flour of pulses and cereals), kebab chini (tailed pepper), poppy seeds, nutmeg, mace and papaya, which is used to tenderize the meat. The use of poppy seeds, or posto dana, is common in West Bengal, and perhaps because of their geographical proximity to Bihar, there has resulted a cross-cultural evolution of this dish, further enhancing its flavour. In her article, Tirmizi also writes that during the Partition of 1947, many Bihari Muslims migrated to Pakistan, taking with them their culture, language and their kebab recipe.[13] That is why it is such a popular street food dish in Lahore. It is this flavourful kebab that made Nawab Wajid Ali Shah of Lucknow, who was losing his teeth, order his khansamas to make him a kebab that could be consumed easily. It resulted in the delicious and popular galawati kebab of Lucknow. But I can guarantee that once you eat a Bihari kebab, there will be no turning back.

It's strange then to think that Bihar, a land that is predominantly associated with vegetarian dishes, that gave birth to Jainism and Buddhism, a place that finds a mention in the Ramayana and the Mahabharata, also serves some of the best kebabs in the country. For people unfamiliar with Bihar, its food repertoire is often limited to litti chokha – a simple, fuss-free but delectable dish which is made of whole wheat-flour (litti) dumplings, stuffed with sattu and cooked on charcoal and served with chokha, a pungent dip of aubergine, tomato, potato and mustard oil. But Bihari cuisine is so much more than just this.

Bihar's relationship with kebabs goes all the way back to the thirteenth century when the Delhi Sultanate brought along with it Islam and meat dishes to a predominately vegetarian population. The famous Moroccan traveller, Ibn Battuta, mentions in his *Rihlat Ibn Battuta* (*Travels of Ibn Battuta*), that the kebab was an integral part of the Indian royalty's diet as early as 1200 CE.[14] According to food historian and author S.S. Prasad, it is perhaps Sher Shah Suri who brought the kebab to Bihar, because the mention of this delicacy in history books starts during and after his rule.[15] The Bihari kebab is different because it often uses game meat and the pieces are usually bigger than the usual minced-meat variety. Another unique feature is the use of sattu and poppy seeds, which is not a common ingredient in other kebabs. Bihari kebabs are slim cuts and the meat that is used comes from the rear legs of the animal, which is usually rich in flavour. They are also a bit spicier and do not require any dip with them.

In 2017, when I was doing research for my TEDx talk at Jamia Millia Islamia, I came to the realization that kebabs connect the whole world. Early human beings ate something like the kebab – meat grilled over an open fire, but without the delectable spices that we have now. The kebab, as we know it now, has its origins in the Middle East, where it is known as 'kabobs'. This humble dish of grilled meat and/or grilled vegetables or paneer can be found in all parts of the world with its own unique cultural inflections. As it travelled, it gained its own twists in flavour and presentation. Every culture has its own versions and names. From chapli, tawa, boti to kakori and galawati kebab, among many others, Indians alone have many different kinds of meat and vegetable kebabs.

Before moving to Delhi in 2011, I too was unaware of the many varieties of kebabs on offer. I never realized that there was a difference between boti kebab and seekh kebab. Even the concept of green chutney as an accompaniment with kebabs was novel, because back home we would just squeeze a dash of fresh lime juice or vinegar on the meat and pair it with chopped onions. The kebab's versatility, its sheer punch of flavour, its simple and effortless presentation is what makes me its ardent champion. The kebab brings people together, evoking a sense of community because of its familiarity. And that is why it makes the perfect treat on Eid.

As the evening moon would rise in the inky sky, the housemaids would light up the lanterns and Bilqis Manzil would flicker to life. The day's celebration would come to an end by the evening, and close family members would gather for the night's feast. The children would all receive *eidi* (money given during Eid) from their elders. The denomination of the currency would depend on how close the visitor was to the family, but I don't remember getting anything lower than a ₹20 note.

At night, we would all gather in the *aangan* to eat kebabs right off the skewers. I don't ever remember the kebab plate reaching the dining hall or the table. The unsaid tradition was to eat it hot and fresh, right off the flame. More often than not, I could be found with a whole skewer in hand. These are the moments I miss in my hectic city life. The simple charm of gathering with my family while talking over delicious plates of kebabs and biryani, is a captivating memory to hold on to.

## Recipe

Serves: 4 to 5
Cooking time: 30 minutes
Preparation time: 12 hours for marination

### Ingredients

#### *For the kebab garam masala (A)*

- 2 tsp kebab chini
- 2 tsp fennel
- 2 star anise
- 4 tsp whole black peppercorns
- 2 cloves
- ½ tsp nutmeg
- 1 tsp mace
- 10 green cardamoms
- 6 black cardamoms
- 2 tbsp coriander seeds
- 2 tbsp cumin seeds
- 12 dried red chillies

#### *For the kebabs*

- 1½ kilogram buff chunk or lamb, thinly sliced and pounded
- ¾ cup yoghurt
- ⅓ cup raw papaya with skin, finely grated
- ¾ cup fried onions
- 4 tsp ginger, freshly grated
- 4 tsp garlic, chopped
- 1 tsp nutmeg powder
- 1 tsp cinnamon powder

- 1½ tsp cumin powder, roasted
- 2 tsp red chilli powder, or to taste
- 2 tsp poppy seeds
- 4 tsp Bihari kebab garam masala
- ¾ cup mustard oil (optional)
- Salt to taste
- Ghee for grilling

## Method

1. On a hot pan, dry roast all the whole spices (A) till they release their fragrance. Then, grind it into a fine powder to make the kebab garam masala.
2. In a clean bowl, add all the leftover ingredients, oil and four teaspoons of the kebab garam masala. Mix it to a smooth paste and massage it properly on to the meat.
3. Let the meat sit for at least 10–12 hours.
4. Stick the meat on to an iron skewer and grill on an open flame, ensuring to apply ghee at regular intervals till the kebabs are cooked. If you don't have a barbeque, grill the kebabs on a normal pan.
5. Serve with fresh onion slices and green chutney.

# 6

# Nihari

ON THE SECOND MORNING of Eid-ul-Zuha (Bakrid), Bilqis Manzil would be in a state of chaos. We'd wake up early, have our baths and begin with the food prep, cutting and chopping vegetables and spices, setting up the dastarkhān, arranging soup bowls, laying out the plates, spoons and ladles. I would be running endless errands from the kitchen to the dining area. I looked forward to this moment every year, because it was all for food. The Eid special breakfast of champions – nihari with khamiri roti.

This hearty dish is always eaten one day after the *qurbani* because it needs a lot of prep and cooking time. In our home, this process would begin on the first day of Eid, after the meat was sorted, cleaned and marinated. The meat would be braised and placed in a *daigh* (a large, round pot), sealed with a flour paste and then left to simmer in the aromatic and delightfully spicy essence of masalas on the woodfire in the *aangan*. This entire process helps the meat absorb the masalas and positively makes it melt in your mouth. After a few hours, the lid is removed and then – magic!

Nihari, a meat stew, is always eaten in the morning. In fact, the word 'nihari' comes from the Arabic word '*nahaar*', meaning day. The royals would eat nihari after their sunrise prayers and then nap until their afternoon prayers.

And so, at 9.30 a.m. we would gather in the dining hall next to the *aangan* to enjoy the fruit of the previous night's labour. Chote Mamu had a naanbai (a cook who makes naans), who'd make fresh and soft khamiri roti to pair with the nihari. He'd give the naanbai a count of how many rotis to make as well as the ingredients in big bags. Early the next morning, the naanbai would come around with fresh, hot khamiri roti wrapped in newspaper and rolled in a bedsheet to keep them warm.

I have not met anyone who doesn't like this bowl exploding with flavours, meat and shorba (soup). The secret behind a good bowl of nihari is its slow-cooking on a low flame and, of course, the fifty-odd spices that go into its making. The Mughal royals loved it, my family loves it and even Zorawar Kalra, the king of Indian cuisine and owner of Massive Restaurants, loves it. In one of our conversations at Farzi Café, Gurugram, he confessed that the one dish he could have for breakfast, lunch and dinner was nihari.

Nihari was a popular dish in the Mughal kitchens as it kept people warm through the brutal winter months. It was also believed to have medicinal value, curing issues related to the sinus. Surprisingly, however, this rather rich dish was not created for the royals. Nihari was actually the go-to dish for the labourers of Old Delhi who were engaged in the intensive constructions of Shahjahanabad. Packed with protein, a bowl of nihari, or bone broth, first thing in the morning would give them the much-needed energy to start their day.[16]

When I was last in Lucknow, I found myself at Rahim's in Phoolwali Gali, Chowk – a small food joint located right next to Tunday Kababi, which is an institution in itself. Over a bowl of nihari, which was less red and also less *rogan* (fatty) and lighter than its Delhi cousin, I learned another very similar version of the nihari's genesis. In 1784, the city was struck by a devastating famine. To fight the situation and help the citizens make money, the reigning nawab, Asaf-ud-Daula, ordered the construction of a monument – that would in later years become its most iconic and popular tourist spot – the Bara Imambara. The workers who were employed in the project were paid in kind – a bowl of nihari in lieu of their services. This wholesome and hearty dish was created to serve a starving populous and a heaving workforce. It is said that the construction and the famine both lasted for 11 years. One can only imagine people standing in queue with a bowl in hand, waiting for their turn to be served what would perhaps be their only meal of the day. While many believe that the nihari originated in Old Delhi during the late eighteenth century, during the last days of the Mughal empire, one clue that points to more humble origins lies in the dish itself. To add body to nihari, a thin paste of wheat flour is used, which indicates that it was originally a poor man's meal, since the more royal dishes were usually cooked in cream and had additional dried fruit.

Despite competing historical origin stories, most agree that this dish is usually eaten in the morning because it releases energy slowly, burns fat and allows for high energy and fewer food cravings later in the day. Now, however, it is common to find nihari being sold throughout the day. Even at home today, often when Ammi is not in the mood to cook or when Shabi is in no mood to eat home-cooked food, he just walks over to Hauz Rani market and brings home steaming plates of nihari and khamiri roti or naan.

Today, one can find nihari everywhere, but if I had to pick my top three spots to eat this dish in Delhi, I'd say Haji Shabrati Nihari Wale and Saeed Nihari in Old Delhi, and, of course, Javed Famous Nahari in Okhla. One year during Ramzan, Shabi and I drove to Okhla to indulge ourselves in a food fest. That evening, Zakir Nagar market was so packed that there was barely any room to walk without bumping into people. Although our aim was to eat nihari, we stopped at many places along the way, trying out the various fares on offer, each one as delicious as the next. By the time we got to Javed Famous Nahari – an old joint that specializes in nihari and nothing else – we had worked up quite an appetite. The board outside said they used real ghee and not oil to prepare the dish, which was a real draw because anything cooked in ghee tastes better than things cooked in oil or any other kind of fat. Inside, on the ground floor, three naanbais sat around a tandoor churning out fresh, hot rotis. We went upstairs to the seating area and quickly ordered a plate of nihari and four rotis, and half-an-hour later (this was peak rush hour) we were served our food. The wait was well worth it. All it took was one bite for us to realize why this shop was called 'famous' – it was simply divine. Two servings later, Shabi and I staggered home, stuffed, satisfied and powered by the joy of excellent nihari. Sadia Dehlvi, in her book *Jasmine and Jinns,* talks about her love for nihari growing up at Shama Kothi, and she tells us a little secret behind a good nihari, which is to add leftover nihari or 'taar' in the fresh batch.[17]

Whenever I visited my cousins and other relatives in Old Delhi, it was common to have nihari on Sundays. My cousin brothers, Shadab and Akka Bhaijan, accompanied by a house help carrying a big utensil, would set off to Haji Shabrati Nihari Wale and bring back fresh nihari with khamiri roti. In a way, nihari was a Sunday tradition in our family. From Bilqis Manzil and Fazal Manzil in Sasaram to our home in Ramgarh, we were tied together by this early Sunday morning breakfast ritual. And I love the fact that it was our love for food that created this tradition.

## Recipe

Serves: 4
Cooking time: 70 to 90 minutes

### Ingredients

- 1 kg mutton or buffalo shanks
- 4 tsp fennel seeds
- 2 tsp cumin seeds
- 2-inch cinnamon stick
- 4 tsp dried ginger powder
- 1 blade of mace
- ½ tsp nutmeg
- 5 green cardamoms
- 3 black cardamoms
- 4 bay leaves
- 12–14 cloves
- 15 whole black pepper
- 1 cup ghee
- 2 tbsp ginger–garlic paste
- 2 tsp red chilli powder
- 1 tsp Kashmiri chilli powder
- Water as per requirement
- ½ cup whole-wheat flour
- Salt to taste
- Freshly chopped coriander, caramelized onions, green chillies and lemon slices

### Method

1. On a griddle, dry roast the whole spices and ginger powder on a low flame. Make sure you do not burn it.

2. Grind the spices to a fine powder. I'd advise using a mortar and pestle, but feel free to use a mixer grinder. This is the nihari masala.
3. Take a big, deep vessel and pour in the ghee. Heat the ghee and add the ginger–garlic paste, cooking it till the rawness disappears or till it turns pale brown.
4. Add both the chilli powders and meat pieces, and sauté on a high flame for 4–5 minutes.
5. Lower the flame and add the nihari masala with salt.
6. Properly coat the meat with the spices and cook for 10–12 minutes.
7. Pour 4–5 cups of water, bring it to a boil and let it cook on a very low flame till the meat is soft and starts to fall off the bone.
8. If you are using a pressure cooker, cook for 2–3 whistles and turn off the flame.
9. Let the dish boil on a low flame even after the required number of pressure cooker whistles or when the meat is properly cooked.
10. Roast the whole-wheat flour on a very low flame till it turns pale brown and then let it cool.
11. Add water to the whole-wheat flour and make a slurry out of it. Pour it into the vessel in which the nihari is being cooked.
12. Adjust the consistency of the gravy as per your requirement, but, traditionally, it should neither be too thick nor thin.
13. Leave it to simmer for 10–12 minutes and then take it off the flame.
14. Let it rest for an hour. This will mature the flavour of the nihari.
15. Serve hot with caramelized onions, freshly chopped coriander and chillies as toppings. Drizzle lemon juice over it.
16. Nihari goes wonderfully with hot naan.

# 7

# Nizam's Chicken Kathi Roll

IN 2002, WE DID something different for Eid. Instead of going to Nanna's house in Sasaram, my parents decided to change things up and go to Kolkata instead to meet Naima Chachijaan (my aunt) and all my younger cousins. *'Iss baar* Eid *pe* Calcutta *chalte hai, har baar kya* Sasaram *jaana* (Let's go to Calcutta this time instead of your mother's house),' Abbi had said to Ammi. Even though our opinion did not matter, my brother Shabi and I excitedly nodded our assent. We had never been to Kolkata before and the very thought was exciting.

I remember waking up at dawn, sleepily getting ready to catch the early morning train. Abbi and Ammi were fasting, but my brother and I had a bite before setting off; Muslims are exempt from fasting during travels. There was no direct train to Kolkata from Ramgarh, so we had to travel to Ranchi, about two hours away. We stacked our bulging suitcases, stuffed with festive Eid clothes – Ammi's bright and shimmering suits and our chikankari kurta pyjamas – into Abbi's office car, a small white Maruti 800. The road from Ramgarh to Ranchi always thrilled Shabi and me because it passed by valleys, ravines and mountains. If you left early in the winters or during the monsoons, there was a high likelihood of spotting a rainbow or finding yourself driving through clouds.

Ten hours and many comic books later, we reached Howrah Station in Kolkata. Everywhere there were shiny yellow taxis, honking loudly and causing great traffic jams. In Ramgarh we never took taxis and thought they were usually for the ultra-rich folk who would book them for the day. The mode of local transport was a kind of small jeep, known as a 'trekker', that could ferry 12 people. But it was more common to find at least 20 passengers hanging on for dear life. So imagine our excitement when Abbi hailed one of those gleaming yellow cabs to Chachijaan's house. We were wide-eyed at the bustle of this new, big city. The streets were crammed with taxis, people, busses, *hathgadis* (hand-drawn rickshaws) and trams. The great colonial buildings and monuments looked straight out of the old movies and my history books. Everything here was throbbing with life and it felt like a fantastic adventure.

My father, who was fluent in Bengali and a pro at navigation, got us to Chachijaan's house in time for iftar. We made our way to the dastarkhān and feasted on a huge meal that included biryani, a dish usually served at lunch. After the meal, the women and men went into separate rooms for namaz. Following that, the children went off to play while the adults drank tea and caught up with each other.

In the evening, Chachu took us to the nearby market to experience Kolkata and its old-world charm. We made our way through the narrow lanes and wound up at Nizam's, one of the oldest and most iconic food joints in the New Market area. It is considered the best place in the city for kathi rolls or what is more famously known as a Nizam's roll. Cooks roll out the maida dough into round rotis, shallow fry them on a flat hot tawa till they are crispy and then crack an egg on top. This is then topped with kebabs and crunchy onions, and Nizam's special green chutney. They are called 'kathi rolls' because a skewer in Bengali is called '*kati*'. The kebab, which is stuffed into the crispy roti, comes straight off the skewers, hence the name. Since it was the month of Ramzan, Nizam's was completely packed. The guy making the rolls was working like a machine; I don't think he stopped even once for a breather. I felt sorry for him because he was directly in front of the heat, which must have been rather uncomfortable. My Chachu, who has lived in Kolkata for close to 30 years and has been going to Nizam's since he was young, tells me that the flavour has remained unchanged. Chachu's friend, Ahmed Uncle, told me that the reason these rolls are famous is because the Nizam's franchise was the first to sell kathi rolls across Kolkata. Today, Nizam's can be found in multiple places across Kolkata and other cities as well.

The best part of eating a kathi roll is the crispy flaky paratha and the tangy sauce that comes with the juicy meat. Your palate feels confused with so many textures and flavours touching all your food chords at once. Each roll comes wrapped in paper, so you've got to carefully unwrap it with every bite as you dive in.

In Kolkata there is almost a consensus about how the kathi roll was born, and it goes something like this. There is no doubt that when the Mughals introduced kebabs to this part of the world, they were a complete hit. Everybody loved them and adapted them to their own tastes. And the British were no exception. They loved the flavour of kebabs, but were uncomfortable using their hands to eat them. A master chef at Nizam's came up with the idea of stuffing the kebabs inside a flaky roti to make it easier for them to eat. Voila! The kathi roll was born. Even though this story is quite popular in Kolkata, there is no written document to back it up. But how does that matter?

Kathi rolls are a beloved snack in Kolkata and around India. In a food survey by *Outlook*, it is mentioned that the kathi roll is the city's second most famous delicacy (a distant second to machher jhol, or fish curry)[18], and Jaideep Mazumdar in *Swarajya* (2018) reports that roughly 1.2 lakh kathi rolls are consumed by Kolkata folk every day.[19]

Today, there are a thousand variations of rolls and wraps with different kinds of rotis and stuffings, including butter chicken kathis and Chinese spring roll kathis. But my heart still sings for the original one that I had as a kid with my uncle in Kolkata.

---

## Recipe

Serves: 4 to 6
Cooking time: 70 minutes + 60 minutes for marination

### Ingredients

#### *For the chicken kebabs*

- 500 gm chicken
- 1 tsp black salt
- 1 tsp lemon juice
- ½ tsp garam masala
- 1 tsp Kashmiri red chilli powder
- ½-inch ginger, crushed
- 2–3 garlic cloves, crushed
- 3½ tbsp curd
- 1 tbsp mustard oil

- Salt to taste
- 1 piece of charcoal
- 1 tbsp ghee

### *For the paratha*

- 450 gm all-purpose flour
- 1 tbsp powdered sugar
- 2 tbsp oil
- Warm water to knead
- Salt to taste

### *For the stuffing*

- 200 gm onion, sliced
- 1 green chilli, chopped
- Green chutney
- Lemon juice as per taste
- Chaat masala as per taste

### Method

1. Cut the chicken into small chunks. Feel free to use either chicken breast or thighs. (I would advise thighs.)
2. Marinate the chicken in black salt, lemon juice, garam masala, Kashmiri red chilli, crushed ginger and garlic, curd and mustard oil.
3. Adjust salt as per taste.
4. Place a burnt piece of charcoal inside a small steel bowl, and then place this inside the bowl with chicken. Pour ghee on top of the charcoal piece. Cover the lid and let it sit for 5–7 minutes.
5. Take the charcoal out of the bowl and let the chicken marinate for another 60 minutes.

6. Put the chicken on to the wooden or iron skewers and cook them on a grill pan till they are perfectly cooked and have charred marks on their surface.
7. In another bowl, add all-purpose flour and oil. Knead them together till the consistency is like breadcrumbs. Add salt and sugar and knead with warm water till the mixture turns into a soft and stretchy dough.
8. Drizzle a little oil on the dough's surface and keep it covered for 30–45 minutes.
9. Divide the dough into equal balls and let them rest once again for 10 minutes.
10. Roll the dough out and then shape it into a coil. Then, roll the dough out again. This will give the flakiness to the paratha.
11. Heat a flat tawa and apply some ghee on it. Cook the paratha on both sides till it becomes crispy and golden.
12. Take it off the heat.
13. Put the onion, chaat masala, lemon juice, green chilli and chicken kebabs in the middle of the paratha. Top it up with green chutney and wrap in a paper.
14. Serve hot with extra chutney or mayonnaise.

# 8

# Murgh Musallam

HOW IMPORTANT A ROLE did food play in our social lives? I'll tell you.

Chote Mamu once told me a story about a wedding party that broke up at the last moment because there was no murgh musallam on the menu! All relatively well-off families would almost always serve murgh musallam and makhuti (a sweet dish made out of lentils) to all the *baratis* (groom's family). This groom's party was aghast that the bride's side could not honour their small request of serving this dish. It was sheer callousness! How could they be sure that this carelessness would not persist after the wedding? And so it was called off. This story may sound absurd, but such is the madness of people. As a child, I thought this story was hilarious and would often ask Chote Mamu to repeat it.

So, what is this wedding deal-breaker of a dish?

Murgh musallam holds a very special place in Indian culinary history. Its unique technique and unparalleled texture made this the centrepiece of an exotic Awadhi dastarkhān. There is a mention of this dish in the *Ain-i-Akbari* as '*musamman*', which is perhaps why it became '*musallam*' (whole). In fact, according to Bisma

Tirmizi, murgh mussallam is one of the 30 dishes mentioned in the *Akbarnama*, written by the famous Navratan Abul Fazl.[20] Colleen Taylor Sen, in her book *Feasts and Fasts*, writes that in the *Ain-i-Akbari* the same dish was made by removing the bones of the bird, but keeping it intact, marinating it in curd and spices. This bird is then stuffed with rice, nuts, minced meat and boiled eggs before it is baked with butter and spices.[21]

There are mentions of this dish across the country. In an interview with Anoothi Vishal, Salma Husain, acclaimed author and food historian, says that references to a similar kind of roasted chicken can be found in Tamil literature from the third century BCE and that this was also among the sacrificial meat dishes served by King Dashratha in the Ramayana.[22]

One of the reasons this dish isn't quite easily available is because of the technique involved. The original recipe requires the removal of the chicken's bones through the bird's neck, a tricky manoeuvre that can be hard to pull off. Perhaps that is why Ammi always made it with the bones intact. But despite this bottleneck, murgh musallam is a delightful dish. The process requires a whole chicken to be marinated in curd, ginger–garlic paste, stuffed with boiled eggs and seasoned with spices like saffron, cinnamon, cloves, poppy seeds, cardamom and chilli, along with some dry fruit. Once marinated for one to two hours, it undergoes a slow-cooking process till the meat becomes tender and melts in your mouth. It is usually a dry dish served whole on the table with a garnish of silver leaves.

Digvijaya Singh's celebrated cookbook, and also one of my favourites, *Cooking Delights of The Maharajas*, consists of 164 authentic recipes of dishes made for the royals. One of them is murgh mussallam in which he deals with the intricacies and the complexities of the dish.[23] His stuffing recipe is also similar to

Ammi's, which includes cashews, poppy seeds, chopped almonds, raisins and spices. Ammi does not add extra milk, water and curd for the gravy, whereas the cookbook instructs that you do. While I was doing my research on this dish, I stumbled upon variations where the chicken is also stuffed with minced mutton or hard-boiled eggs.

My family would make this dish on special occasions, such as Eid or if there was a guest who was coming to meet us after ages. The *aangan* of Bilqis Manzil was large enough to set up a rustic-style kitchen where my aunts and cooks would prepare food on an open fire. Ammi, who learned this dish from Nanna, always used a big dish to mix all the spices and the curd together. She'd then coat the chicken well and leave it to marinate. Once marinated, the chicken would be put in an earthen pot, tightly sealed and placed over a slow flame for 45 to 60 minutes. In our home in Ramgarh, this process would get a modern touch, where she'd marinate the chicken and either cook it in the oven or a deep vessel on the stove.

This dish is Ammi's second masterpiece after biryani, and it's always a joint effort with both my parents pitching in. Ammi would weigh all the spices and make the marinade, while Abbi would ensure that the meat was clean and the stuffing of dry fruit, boiled egg and caramelized onions was ready. They'd then tie the chicken with kitchen thread and place it in the oven. Watching them cook this difficult dish together like a team was quite a therapeutic experience for me. The whole chicken was washed a few times and cleansed properly, and then the bird was massaged with the marinade so that it was properly coated. This is a delicate process ('*Nazakat,*' as Ammi would say).

One Christmas, Baishali, a friend of mine, invited a few of us to her house for dinner. Being the in-house chef, I was, by default, given charge of rustling up a few dishes and I decided to take the opportunity to serve my friends murgh musallam, because it is quite similar to the traditional Christmas roast chicken. The mood was festive; Baishali's husband, Imna, had decorated the house beautifully and carols were playing in the background as I cooked. I cleaned the whole chicken with its cavity intact quite nicely, and since there was no oven at her place, I had to use a deep vessel instead. All the knowledge and skills I used that day I learned from my parents.

Since I was cooking for 14 people, I had to prepare and marinate two chickens. It took almost 60 minutes for my birds to get nicely marinated and the only thing left to do was stuff the chicken cavity with onions, eggs and dry fruit, and tie it neatly before setting it over the fire. My friend Srijan walked into the kitchen just as I was stuffing the eggs into the chicken's cavity. He was stumped! For the remainder of the evening, he called me a monster for putting the egg back into the chicken!

Even though my friends tell me it is the best thing they've ever eaten, murgh musallam always reminds me of Chote Mamu. Whenever there was a fancy neighbourhood wedding we were invited to, Chote Mamu would ensure Shabi and I got dressed in our best before we'd ride with him on his black motorbike to the venue. Shabi and I usually had only one objective – to eat as much as possible, and if we happened to be at a wedding where they were serving murgh musallam, we'd pounce on it immediately. Chote Mamu also didn't take lightly to the murgh musallam story he had told us. At his own wedding, he ensured it was the first thing on the menu.

## Recipe

Serves: 4
Cooking time: 150 to 180 minutes

### Ingredients

- 1 kg whole chicken
- 3 tbsp curd
- 1 tbsp red chilli powder
- ½ tsp Kashmiri red chilli powder
- 1 tbsp coriander powder
- 1 tsp garam masala powder
- ½ tbsp cumin powder
- 1 tbsp ginger–garlic paste
- Salt to taste
- 2 eggs, hard boiled
- ¼ cup almonds, fried
- 15 cashew nuts, fried
- 2 tbsp raisins, fried
- 2 medium onions, fried
- ½ cup ghee
- Water

### Method

1. Wash and pat dry the whole chicken. Then make a few deep gashes on the chicken's skin.
2. In another bowl, mix curd, red chilli powder, Kashmiri red chilli powder, coriander powder, garam masala, cumin powder, ginger–garlic paste and salt into a smooth paste.

3. Place the chicken in this bowl and give it a nice rub with the marinade. Let it sit for 60–90 minutes.
4. Stuff the chicken's cavity with the boiled eggs, dry fruit and fried onions before sealing it with a string.
5. In a deep pan, add some ghee and cook the chicken on a high flame for 8–10 minutes on all sides.
6. Sprinkle some water in the pan, cover and cook the chicken on a low flame for 20 minutes.
7. After 20 minutes, check if the chicken is well-cooked. Either poke a toothpick or a knife near the thigh and if it comes out clean, your dish is ready. Once the chicken is fully cooked, take it out and serve with rice, paratha or by itself.

# 9

# Akhti

OUR VISITS TO SASARAM were never complete without us stopping by at Fazal Manzil. Just like Bilqis Manzil, Fazal Manzil was a sprawling bungalow that housed 10 families of the Hussain clan. It had two huge *aangans*, a well and three kitchens to cook meals for its many occupants. Dadi (my paternal grandmother), who was another great cook of her time, passed away when I was just four years old, so my memories of time spent with her are a blur. Mostly, I remember my aunt, uncle and first cousins living in this rambling mansion. Shabi and I oddly called my aunt 'Abbu-Ammi'. Ammi tells me that we did so because as children we used to call her Abbu ki Ammi (mother of my uncle), even though she was Abbu's wife. Eventually, logic dawned upon us and we removed the 'ki', thereby shortening it to Abbu-Ammi.

Abbu and Abbu-Ammi would host us with amazing food and lots of stories from the past. Abbu had kept my grandfather's old, rustic hookah, his old walking stick, a big brass plate, a few old wooden boxes and some other artefacts. On the ground floor, there was a large room stuffed with old ornaments and handcrafted furniture from my grandparents' era. My grandfather was never around when I was born, and my grandmother passed away when I was just four. So I didn't really know them, but just going through their furniture and other things made me think that they had a simple yet sophisticated life.

Abbu-Ammi made amazing food, and one particular dish stands out.

One summer at Sasaram, Abbu-Ammi invited us for dinner, and offered us a spread of many different vegetarian and non-vegetarian dishes. Among them was a little-heard-of dish called akhti, a mutton curry with flour dumplings. These dumplings are simply made of wheat, water and salt, and aren't stuffed with vegetables or meat. Truth be told, I had forgotten all about this dish. It was only when I was compiling stories for this book and had asked my parents if there were any special savoury dishes Dadi would make did my mother remind me of Abbu-Ammi's akhti.

I reached out to my cousins, and Akka Bhaijan told me that at Fazal Manzil, all three siblings would sit in a line making the dumplings, while the meat was prepared. I laughed as I pictured my three errant cousins patiently sitting, whining away, as they made the dumplings, and perhaps fighting over the process. Shadab Bhaijan then told me that he remembered helping Dadi make akhti for one of the functions at my parents' wedding.

There are a lot of dishes I ate when I was young that I don't really remember now – blame it on my bad memory, or on the fact that I did not get to eat the same dishes later as an adult. My first cousins Akka Bhaijan, Shadab Bhaijan and Appi would always mention the food made by Dadi.

So when I rang Abbu-Ammi, she was pleasantly surprised by my request for her akhti recipe. Abbu-Ammi had learned this dish from Dadi when she was a young bride. She still makes it as a winter special. In fact, even now her friends and family demand to be hosted for special dinners that include haleem and akhti. Abbu-Ammi is now in her late fifties, and it's a wonder she has the energy to make both these dishes, given how labour-intensive they are. I was glad that she still remembered the dish and could help me with the recipe, because akhti is an endangered dish.

As I noted down the recipe, I realized she was asking me to add garam masala in its powdered form, along with the whole spices, meaning that the dish gets its flavour from all of these spices. She also suggested that I add roasted cumin and coriander powder in the dish and to keep some cumin powder aside to sprinkle on top afterwards. This is important as these spices play a vital role in our physical well-being.

Sanchari Pal in her article 'Food Fit for Royalty: So What Did The Mughal Emperors Eat for Dinner?' writes, 'It was also not uncommon for the shahi khansama [chief cook] to consult with the shahi hakim [chief physician] while planning the royal menu, making sure to include medicinally beneficial ingredients.'[24] Akhti calls for cardamom, both black and green. Green cardamom helps with digestive disorders and perhaps this could be one reason that Mughals often used it in their dishes. The *Nimmatnama-i-Nasiruddin-Shahi* also has dishes which utilize cardamom as one of the spices. But if we go further back in history, to the eleventh century, we'll find the mention of green cardamom in *Manasollasa*, a twelfth-century Sanskrit text touted to be one of the first recipe books in India. In fact, green cardamom is the only spice, along with black pepper, which is native to Kerala. Cardamom is quintessential to Indian food and beverages, and is so versatile that it can be used in both sweet and savoury dishes, from the famous paan to kheer.

There is very little evidence or trail of how this dish came to be, evolved or was enjoyed. There is very little on the internet too. When I reached out to Abu Sufiyan, Chairman of Tareekh,

Arts and Culture Trust, and a friend, who is trying to restore the stories of Old Delhi, he told me that one couldn't find this dish anywhere in Shahjahanabad (Old Delhi). Challenging his word, I scoured the *gallis* of the old city but in vain. Abu Sufiyan was right. Akhti was extinct in the city that had once, perhaps, given birth to it.

Soma Hashmi in her article 'A Brief History of Mughlai Food in Agra, India' says, 'Mughal food was originally invented by fusing existing Persian and Indian cuisines. The Mughal Empire attained many of its attributes from the Persians, including language, which is why several Mughlai dishes have a typical Persian ring to them.'

Akhti has an English name – Indian Mutton Curry with Dumplings – but that simply doesn't have the same ring to it. The internet does not really have any answer on the history of Akhti, apart from one article by Masha Hassan ('Rediscovering Akhti, A Lost Dish of India', *Epicure and Culture*, 31 July 2017). When I reached out to her, she told me that the first time she had akhti was when she was just two years old, and it was her grandmother who used to make it. Unlike my family, Masha said akhti was popular in her house during Ramzan. When I asked her if she could guess the origin, she wasn't sure, but said it was possibly from Bihar, where her family was originally from. This would make sense, since my family is from Bihar too and my aunt also believes it is a local dish. I'm not sure about the origin of this dish, but I feel like I have finally found a connection to my Dadi through my Abbu-Ammi, although I wish I'd had the chance to experience her cooking first-hand.

As the years went by, my uncles and aunts moved out of Fazal Manzil, selling their share of the property. The once-bustling home shrank to a small space that housed three families, which included Abbi and his two elder brothers. Eventually, it was just Abbu and Abbu-Ammi left in the house, sheltering the stories and recipes of the past, so that they live on in someone else's home.

---

## Recipe

Serves: 4
Cooking time: 120 to 150 minutes

### Ingredients

- 1 kg mutton, cut in small pieces
- 8 large onions
- ½ cup curd
- ½ cup mustard oil for frying
- 5 tbsp ginger–garlic paste
- 2 tbsp turmeric powder
- 2 tsp garam masala powder
- 2 tsp red chilli powder
- 4 bay leaves
- 2 tbsp coriander seeds
- 1 tbsp whole black pepper corns
- 5 black cardamoms
- 7 green cardamoms
- 2 inches cinnamon
- 1 blade of mace
- 2 tbsp + 3 tbsp cumin seeds
- 2 star anise
- Salt to taste
- Freshly chopped coriander, caramelized onions, green chillies and lemon slices to garnish and serve

### *For the dumplings*

- 2 cups whole-wheat flour
- 2 tbsp ghee
- ½ tbsp salt
- Water

## Method

1. When buying the meat, ask for pieces from either the shoulder or the leg, and get it chopped into small chunks. Wash and rinse the mutton pieces and pat them dry.
2. Knead the flour into a nice, tight dough for the dumplings and let it rest.
3. In another bowl, marinate the mutton pieces with three tablespoons of ginger–garlic paste, turmeric powder and salt.
4. Chop the onions and fry them in oil till they turn golden brown.
5. In a pan, dry roast the coriander seeds, black pepper, bay leaves, black and green cardamoms, cinnamon, mace, star anise and two tablespoons of cumin seeds. Grind this into a fine powder. A mortar and pestle is preferred, but if you don't have one, a mixer grinder will do the job.
6. In a big, deep vessel (or a pressure cooker if you don't have enough time), heat the oil and add the marinated mutton pieces with the spice mix that we just made.
7. Sauté on a high flame for 8–10 minutes without burning the meat or spices. Ensure that the meat is properly coated with spices and oil.
8. Toss in the caramelized onions and chilli powder, according to taste.

9. Lower the flame and add the curd, which is to be whisked, and cook for 10–12 minutes.
10. Add water according to how thick or thin you like your gravy. Cover the lid and let it cook for three whistles. If you are not using a pressure cooker, then cook till the meat is tender.
11. While the meat is cooking, roll out the dough and separate them into small dumplings. Keep them small and bite-sized. You can cut them out in shapes as well. The most common shape, also popular in my house, is the flower shape.
12. Once the meat is cooked and tender, take it out of the gravy and shred it using a fork. Toss the meat back in the gravy, mix and cook again for 10 minutes.
13. Add the dumplings in the gravy, poaching them till they are cooked well. You can take one out and cut into it to check whether it is cooked properly or not.
14. Cook over a low flame for 10 minutes once again and then add the garam masala.
15. Serve hot with a garnish of coriander leaves, chillies, lemon juice and some extra roasted cumin powder.

# 10

# Paan

IF THERE WAS ONE thing I have never seen Nanna without, it is her silver *paandaan* (a box that held the betel leaves and other ingredients to make paan). She treated it with great care and respect. It would be an understatement to say Nanna loved her paan. She would make it herself, cut the leaf, spreading katha (catechu) and chuna (lime stone) with a black stick, adding her spices, folding the leaf into a triangle and then, finally, putting it into her mouth. It was nothing less than art. Usually, she'd quickly eat one after breakfast, but in the winters, she'd sit in the *aangan,* out in the sun, and leisurely make her paan, while all her grandkids ran around her. When Nanna was young, a bride would get a *paandaan* and *ugaaldaan* (spit box) at her wedding. It was seen as a sign of royalty and a part of *tehzeeb* (refined culture).

Ammi still has her silver *paandaan,* but she has never used it; it is still as new as it was when she got married. According to Abbi, Dada and Dadi also loved their paan; their favourite was the Bangla patta from West Bengal – a big and slightly fibrous leaf, less expensive than the delicate and smaller magahi leaf, which comes from the Magadh region of Bihar. Dadi's favourite place in the house to make paan was on a cot near the *aangan* where she'd get a cool breeze during the summers and warm sun during the winters. On the cot, she'd keep her silver handcrafted *paandaan* to make paan for Dada and herself, and any guests who might drop by and she'd store these rolled paans in a *khaasdaan* (a box especially made to store paans). Abbi also loved paan and in Ramgarh, he would always go to the same shop – Mahendra Paan Wala. This little shop, which started out as just a counter to sell paan, has now turned into a big grocery store. When I asked Abbi about meetha paan, he said that it was not seen in a good light and connoisseurs would never consume this 'lowly' version. This is a modification for the younger generation who want to chew on the leaf but don't enjoy the original flavour of paan. Nana (my maternal grandfather) used to say that one must always offer something to a guest or anyone who has come to our door, otherwise it is the equivalent of going to a morgue. Since food was not always available, it was advised to welcome the guest with paan and pani (water), and if the person does not eat paan, then to offer them elaichi (cardamom).

Paan is a vital part of a traditional Muslim meal. At weddings, it is often the final chapter of the menu similar to fromage (cheese) on a 17-course Italian menu. Paan is often mistaken for betel nut, but it is, in fact, the betel leaf, wrapped around an areca nut. This heart-shaped leaf got its name from the Sanksrit word '*parsa*', which means 'feather' or 'leaf', and the end product is usually filled with chuna (mineral-slaked lime), kattha, supari and other flavouring agents, such as laung (clove) and elaichi. This can be mixed with other ingredients, such as spices, mint, sweetened coconut, dates, gulkand (a sweet preserve of rose petal), cherries, saunf (fennel seeds) and sometimes tobacco.

However, paan isn't just a Muslim offering. It is as old as Indian history itself. According to mythology, the Ayodhya Kand in the Ramayana mentions Lord Ram spending his leisure time chewing betel leaves. In the Bhagvad Gita, Lord Krishna too is depicted chewing betel leaves. On the other hand, Ibn Battuta in his writing mentions the ritual of serving paan in the Mughal courts in Lucknow as a sign of welcome and farewell. This is still a tradition in most homes in India. Your host will never let you leave without offering you a paan from his favourite *panwari* (paan seller). Perhaps paan would qualify as a good example of the Ganga–Jamuni *tehzeeb* (the fusion of Hindu and Muslim culture) of Lucknow, and of a culture that has had an overlap of ingredients, communities and beliefs.

Paan making is a precise art – just a little extra masala can ruin the delicate flavour. Perhaps this is why most people back in the day had their own special ingredients, and made paan according to their specific tastes and preferences, customized based on the mood, environment and occasion.

Paan also holds a great value in Hindu culture. Traditionally, priests receive their *dakshina* (fees) placed on betel leaves and grooms carry betel nuts when they first visit the house of their prospective bride. In the temple of Lord Venkateshwara in Tirupati, the butter which is applied to the forehead of the idol is first wrapped in a betel leaf.

Colleen Taylor Sen in *Feasts and Fasts: A History of Food in India*, notes that, 'Paan became a symbol of hospitality and the focal point of elaborate aristocratic rituals. How one served and ate paan was a marker of sophistication and affluence.' She further quotes a fourteenth-century traveller who says: 'The Indians think the most respectable way to entertain the guest is with the betel leaf. If a person entertains his guests with various kinds of eatables, sherbets, sweetmeats, perfumes and flowers and does not offer betel leaf to them, it means he has not been a good host and guests have not had honour done to them. Similarly, when an important man has to oblige some acquaintance, he offers him a betel leaf.' The affluent even added ground pearls and shells to the chuna in their paan. Even today one can find expensive paans wrapped in silver *varq* in the market.

Ankit Chadha, in his book *Amir Khusrau: The Man in Riddles,* writes about the poet's love for paan and he called it Hindustan's most beautiful delicacy. '*Gala katey, woh choon naa karey/ Aur moonh rakt bahaaye/So pyaari baatein karein/Fikar katha dikhlaaye* (Throat slit, he doesn't make a sound/Blood drips from his mouth/He tells tales like a child/And makes the imagination go wild).'[25]

In fact, this delicacy was made popular by Empress Nur Jahan, who'd use paan as an organic lipstick. Rana Safvi, historian, author and blogger, writes about the steeped relationship of paan in Indian culture on her website. She writes: '... allowance given to women would be called paan kharch. French traveller Niccolao Manucci referred to Mughal Emperor Shah Jahan allocating the revenue of Surat for meeting the paan expenses of his daughter – this meant allowance not as expenses for eating paan!'[26]

Food writer Madhulika Dash describes Jahangir's love for paan in her article, 'Diwali, a festival for Delhi Sultans', saying how '... during Jahangir's reign, a dozen different varieties of sherbert, paan and falooda became part of the feast. The masala for the paan came from Golconda and Mewar, it included pellets made of pure gold and silver, and the fragrant gulkand was made in-house.'[27]

In the *Nimmatnama,* a few images depict Sultan Ghiyas-ud-din Khalji watching the process of paan making. But as Ibn Battuta recounts, it was not just a welcome 'snack'; paan was also offered when guests were done eating their meal since it acts as an oral deodorant and has digestive properties owing to the medicinal properties of the ingredients used.

In her article, Safvi continues, 'Its use in India dates back to 400 BCE. As per ancient books of Ayurveda by Charaka, Sushruta Samhitas and Kashyapa Bhojanakalpa, the practice of chewing betel leaves after meals became common between 75 CE and 300 CE. Vatsyayana, the author of Kamasutra, included the betel leaf in the solah singar [make-up and ornaments of a bride] or the sixteen adornments. Towards the thirteenth century, European traveller Marco Polo recorded betel chewing among kings and nobles in India.'

Truth be told, I have never enjoyed paan. As a child I once tried it at a wedding I attended in Gaya, Bihar. I had no idea how to chew it and I dropped some on my white kurta, immediately staining it. When Ammi saw how I'd ruined my kurta, I was scolded thoroughly. Perhaps it's that unpleasant memory that has tainted my enjoyment of paan forever.

I may not enjoy paan myself, however its stories intrigue me. Paan is an intrinsic part of Indian cuisine. But it was at home, in Bilqis Manzil's *aangan,* watching Nanna lovingly fold her paan, that I first came across it and it sparked my interest. If, like me, you've never liked paan, I'm hoping this delightful poem by Khusrau detailed in *Feasts and Fasts,* will change your mind.

A chew of betel bound in to a hundred leaves,
Came to hand like a hundred-petaled flower.
Rare leaf, like a flower in a garden,
Hindustan's most beautiful delicacy.
Sharp as a rearing stallion's ear
Sharp in both shape and taste,
In sharpness a tool to cut roots
As the Prophet's words tell us
Full of veins with no trace of blood,
Yet from its veins blood races out,

Wondrous plant, for places in the mouth.
Blood comes from its body like a living thing.

---

## Recipe

Serves: 5

### Ingredients

- 4–5 paan patta (betel leaf)
- Chuna (paste of lime-stone powder and water)
- Kattha (paste of catechu and water)
- Sweet powder
- Heera Panna (mix of vegetable and fruit powder)
- Supari (diced betel nut)
- Khajoor (wet dates)
- Hara Patta (green leaves)
- Laung (cloves)
- Silver varq (optional)

### Method

1. Wash the betel leaves and place them on a wet cloth.
2. With the help of a spoon or stick, spread chuna on the leaves.
3. Drizzle a small splash of kattha on top and spread it all over the leaves.
4. Sprinkle some sweet powder, add heera panna and spread and mix it properly all over the leaves.
5. Add a few supari pieces and diced khajoor in the centre of the leaves.
6. Add a small pinch of hara patta.

7. Fold and wrap the leaves into a conical shape.
8. Press some laung into the paan and apply the silver varq. You can eat it fresh or chill it on ice for a bit before eating it.

# Spreading Wings

# 11

# Bheja Fry

THE SUMMER OF 2007 brought with it many big changes. I turned 18 and received my Class 12 board exam results. I had just been accepted at St Xavier's College in Ranchi, Jharkhand, a city almost 60 kilometres away from my house. This meant that I would be moving cities. I packed my bags and left home, feeling weighed down by my heavy backpack. This was the first time I would be living away from home. The day I left, Ammi stood at the door watching me go till I was completely out of her sight. She had packed me a lot of food to eat. Abbi dropped me off at the bus station, gave me ₹3,000 to spend and bid me good luck for my future. The only light at the end of this rather gloomy journey was that Shabi would be waiting for me in Ranchi to take me to the hostel where he was also staying.

When I reached Ranchi, I learned that Shabi wouldn't be able to pick me up because he had some last-minute college work to complete. He asked me to go directly to the hostel, which was called Imdad Manzil, where the caretaker would help me settle in.

Imdad Manzil was a four-storey building that was to be my home for the next three years through college. It was located in a bustling lane with a thriving vegetable market, a DVD rental store and other shops selling electronics, and many small eateries. Situated around our hostel was a mosque, a temple and a gurudwara. There was no moment that one would feel alone or far away from god. During summer, at 4 a.m., I'd wake to the sound of the azan from the mosque. At 5 a.m., bhajans would come alive from the temple near my room. The gurudwara was a little farther away, but often during festivals, we'd head there for prasad.

Shabi introduced me to his friends, who would soon become my friends and 'gang members' as well – Faiz Bhai, Nafees and Nadeem Bhai, who we would often call 'Nadeem Cha' (uncle) because he was slightly older than us. And then college life began. Life was a breeze; all we did was get up, attend classes, come back, eat, watch a movie or play some games and spend our nights talking about the prettiest girl in our respective classes, discussing the philosophies of Che Guevara, Karl Marx and Adam Smith, and the poetry and prose of Ghalib, Manto, Mir Taqi Mir and Machiavelli.

Faiz Bhai, Nadeem Bhai and Nafees had their own room, while Shabi and I shared another. As the youngest in the group, I was at the receiving end of a fair bit of ragging. From cleaning the room, washing the dishes, filling water bottles, cooking and performing other chores, I would have to do it all. But don't get me wrong; it's not like I was being bullied or was depressed about it. Of course, it was annoying to wake up at 5 a.m. to fill buckets with fresh water to cook, drink and bathe, when my classes only began at 6.45 a.m., but in retrospect, it was these very things that made hostel life bearable. We never had time for breakfast, so we'd rush out grabbing a banana or some fruit, and later get a proper bite at one of the many small dhabas near our hostel. But, as a rule of thumb, we always made sure we had dinner together. That was our time to bond and talk about the day.

Hindpiri, where we lived, is a food lover's paradise in Ranchi. At the mouth of the lane there were a few bakeries serving sheermal, naankhatai and pastries; keep walking down the narrow lane and you'll find grocery stores, clothes and tailor shops, and then a line of Muslim restaurants with live counters with fresh rotis right out of the tandoor and juicy kebabs on hot charcoal, all in a whirlwind of aroma and chaos. It was quite impossible to resist once I got a whiff of the dishes being cooked. In fact, Shabi and I often got food packed from these restaurants when we were heading back home to Ramgarh.

Since we were often broke, many times we'd cook our own meals in our room. I'd be the one cooking for all four of us and also the one washing all the dishes. Sometimes they'd complain about the food, even though they'd finish every morsel because they had no other option. Till date, they still take credit for arousing my interest in food and making me who I am! When they wanted a change of palate, Nafees and Faiz Bhai would always go downstairs to a place called Muslim Hotel to grab lunch or dinner.

Muslim Hotel was a ramshackle joint with a few benches and tables, with two guys standing outside and endlessly rolling rotis. The kitchen was installed out in the open but the cooked food would be kept inside, properly covered and waiting in big pots to be ladled out to customers. Even as late as 2007, we would manage a proper meal – a plate of rice with dal and a little gravy – for just ₹5. And so, we went there often, for rotis, tikkis and kebabs. Over time, the owner became familiar with all of us and our spending habits. He knew we'd live comfortably till the twentieth of the month and then be broke for the next 10 days till we received money from home. At times, he would kindly add an extra piece of meat or aloo or bhindi (okra) bhujia to our take-away order of rotis.

One day, I noticed a pan full of spicy bheja fry, cooked to perfection, at the shop's counter. This was perhaps the first time they had made it, and since it looked tempting, I ordered a plate, along with a few rotis. This was not the first time I was eating bheja fry. Ammi made this dish in many different ways, dry and cooked in a pan, cooked with gravy, batter-coated and deep fried like fritters. Muslim Hotel's bheja fry was much spicier and oilier, and I won't say that it was the best. The flavour of brain was usually shadowed by a flood of spices.

Bheja fry literally translates to brain (usually of goat or lamb) cooked in a spicy masala. It can be cooked dry or in a gravy, depending on how one likes it. Brain is a delicate part of an animal, possessing its own distinct buttery flavour, nothing like mutton or red meat.

Today, I've had bheja fry in many places and styles. In Delhi, it appears on the menus of both gourmet restaurants and dhabas. Haji Shabrati Nihari Wale in Old Delhi also has bheja fry on its menu. They usually cook this in a generous serving of salted Amul butter and a fair bit of spices, which gives a gorgeous texture and flavour. In Mumbai, I've eaten it at Mohammad Ali Road – a great place to be during Ramzan for its amazing spicy food; the streets are chock full of people celebrating, and food joints serve lip-smacking dishes late into the night. In Ajmer, while travelling to the shrine of Khwaja Gareeb Nawaz, I was surprised to find eateries serving bheja fry clubbed with khamiri roti, pao or sheermal. Mumbai's version is spicier than its northern offerings, perhaps because of its proximity to Konkan cuisine and spices. I've eaten bheja fry on the streets of Dhaka and Chittagong, where it is usually accompanied by luchis if on the street and paratha, naan or roomali roti at a proper restaurant. It was amazing, but once again, not spiced very differently from the

Indian varieties. I've eaten a dry bheja fry with paratha. The natural moistness of the dish was enough to not require any gravy. And, in Sasaram, Abbu-Ammi or Mami made bheja fry for breakfast in a simpler style, or as a fried fritter by Ammi during Ramzan. Ammi always makes bheja fry using the same masalas that she uses in keema – ginger–garlic paste, cumin powder, coriander powder, garam masala and pepper. Everyone has their own touch and distinct flavour, but I must confess that bheja fry is an acquired taste.

Atul Sikand, friend, food critic and the man behind Asian Hawkers Festival in Delhi, once told me a hilarious account of him eating bheja fry. Atul had been invited to lunch at his Kashmiri friend's house, which included the usual fare – gushtaba, rishta and a few other non-vegetarian dishes. Eventually, he dug into the creamy and rather oily paneer bhurji he had been served. His Punjabi genes approved of this dish. It was only once he'd finished, did he realize what he had eaten. He balked; Atul wouldn't have ever eaten it had he known it was bheja. Finally, when the host's wife asked him what he had liked best, Atul jokingly said 'bheja fry', and so she made him a generous doggy bag and sent him home with it.

Bheja fry has always been a popular street food. It also finds a place on Parsi menus and Irani cafés. I spoke to Kainaz Contractor, chef and owner of Rustom's Parsi Bhonu in Delhi, and she told me that bheja fry used to be a part of her breakfast, but it is not eaten that often any more. She shared two different ways of cooking this dish. One is simple – flavoured with fried onions, green chillies and coriander. The other is popular in Irani cafés and has dhansak masala along with the other seasonings that make it spicy. In her home, unlike mine, bheja fry is a side dish which is paired with pao. At ours, this dish is clubbed with roti.

Sameen Rushdie, in her *Indian Cookery Book*, also mentions bheja fry, describing it as a popular dish in Pakistan and Bangladesh. Bheja fry is also my friend Mohammad Omar's favourite dish. He is from Dhaka, where it is commonly known as brain fry or brain masala. He eats it at least thrice a month, from either BBQ Tonight in Dhanmondi or La Bamba in Uttara. Interestingly, the first time he ever had bheja fry was from a streetside food joint in Mohammadpur, owned by a man from Bihar, called Mostaquim er Chaap. His descriptions of the creaminess and the level of spices in a Bangaldeshi bheja fry always make me salivate. I have promised to cook him this dish when he comes to India, so we can compare which one is better.

Delhi is quite famous for bheja fry, with eateries spread across Old Delhi and West Delhi, where you can have the the dish in gourmet style or in rustic dhaba style. Ibrar Osama, an old collegue, contradicts both of us and says that the flavour of the bheja fry he gets in Mumbai is actually the best.

In 2015, I visited Ranchi for a friend's wedding and went back to Muslim Hotel, curious to see if it was still in business. The place was as full as ever, and I was pleasantly surprised to find that their dish of the day was fresh bheja fry. A tall man wearing a blue-and-white checked lungi was working the giant tawa. I watched him make the dish from start to finish, washing the tawa, frying the onions, then bunging in the masalas with water. The recipe that I am sharing with you is the one I learned that day at Muslim Hotel, as a nod to the owner who always gave us a little extra food with our five-rupee lunch plate.

## Recipe

Serves: 3 to 4
Cooking time: 40 to 45 minutes

### Ingredients

- 3–4 cups water
- 6 tsp turmeric powder
- 3 large bheja (mutton brain)
- 5 tbsp ghee/oil
- 2 large onion
- 2 medium tomatoes
- 1½ tsp red chilli powder
- 1 tsp whole spices powder
- 2 dried chillies
- 2-inch ginger
- 3 green chillies
- Fresh coriander
- Salt to taste

### Method

1. Marinate the bheja in 4 tsp of turmeric and let it rest for 10–15 minutes.
2. Boil 3 cups of water with some salt in it.
3. Put the turmeric-marinated bheja in the water and let it boil for 5–7 minutes. Take the brain out and gently remove the veins. If you're too rough, you may crush the boiled brains.
4. Finely chop onions, tomatoes, ginger, chillies and coriander, and keep aside.

5. In a deep saucepan, heat the ghee/oil and toss in the onions, cooking till they turn translucent.
6. Add tomatoes and green chillies until properly cooked.
7. Add the whole and powdered spices, pour some water and cook till the spices are well-cooked.
8. Add the brains and ginger juliennes into the pan and mix thoroughly.
9. Cook till the oil separates, then add some extra chopped coriander.
10. Bheja fry is ready to serve. Pair it with roomali roti or plain crispy paratha.

12

# Ashraf's Fried Onion Mutton Curry

WHEN MY BROTHER AND his gang graduated, it so happened that they all left our town seeking greener pastures. Nafees was accepted at Delhi's Jawaharlal Nehru University, Nadeem Bhai became a chartered accountant and left for Delhi to begin his practice, Shabi and Faiz Bhai also left for Delhi for their higher studies. Suddenly I found myself left to my own devices.

I moved out of our large double room to a smaller one that had a window overlooking the vegetable market. Often, on Sundays, I would spend time staring out of it at the people haggling for vegetables. Since it was just me, I'd rarely cook. I would get food from the Muslim restaurants downstairs, or simply cook some rice and chicken with a basic onion and curd gravy. I hardly experimented with my food because when I cook, people's feedback is one of my most satisfying takeaways – something that is in short supply when only cooking for oneself. Soon, I began an internship at a media house and my routine changed. I started coming back home only by 7 p.m., and life was no longer filled with vacant hours in my hostel. Things took another pleasant turn when I made a new set of friends; they were Ashraf, Asgar, Moin, Shahbaz and a few others.

Ashraf was a dreamer, lost in his own world, but an amazing friend. He'd lend me money when I was broke; if he bought a new shirt, I'd be the first person to wear it – and he'd liberally use my cologne or borrow my jeans on special occasions. Better still, we were a team when it came to cooking. We'd always been curious about trying out new dishes and cuisines. Soon, we began to establish our own traditions, and one of them was non-vegetarian Friday nights.

Ashraf or Moin would bring home the best pieces of freshly butchered meat after *zuhr* namaz, and one of us would cook it. Gradually others joined our motley crew and we had to shift our kitchen to a bigger room. Arshad, the boy whose room we took over, was a good cook himself, but he was a better singer. While Ashraf and I cooked, Arshad entertained us with beautiful Sufi songs in his deep and soulful voice. Our kitchen was installed in one corner of his room where we had three cartons; one for onions and potatoes, one for spices, and the third one for fresh vegetables. Plates and other utensils were lined up neatly next to these boxes, and beside that, two small, red gas stoves.

One day, bored with the same old mutton curry, Ashraf decided to try something new. Usually, we threw in whole spices into a pressure cooker along with the mutton pieces and cooked them over a low flame for 40 to 45 minutes. That evening, Ashraf wanted to try a smooth, caramelized onion gravy. My job that evening was to assist him in making the masala and keeping an eye on the gas to ensure that nothing burned. After almost 90 minutes of cooking, dinner was ready, and we dug in.

I was stunned by how good Ashraf's mutton curry had turned out. The meat was succulent, almost falling off the bones, the gravy was smooth, enhanced by the richness of the fat. This dish was one-of-its-kind and we all helped ourselves to multiple servings. To this day, I remember the taste of that dish.

The secret to Ashraf's mutton curry lay in the smooth paste of caramelized onions, which gave it a nice, sweet flavour. In the West, people cook red meat and serve it with plum chutney, or a similar sweet and tangy sauce that goes really well with meat. In this case, the caramelized onions work in the same manner in our mutton dish. The British would call this 'mutton curry' because they refer to all gravy-based Indian dishes as 'curry'. The word comes from the French word '*cuire*' meaning, to cook, boil or grill. In fact, the word curry became part of the English vocabulary around the 1300s, with the publication of one of the first English cookery books, *The Forme of Cury*, a project King Richard II commissioned over 180 of his cooks to produce.

The humble onion, when used well, can work wonders on the simplest dishes. Historian Dr Indu Mehta writes that onion finds its mention in the Charaka Samhita (6 BCE) as a bulb with medicinal properties. During World War II, Russian soldiers were so inspired and impressed with the onion that they started using it as an antiseptic to heal their battle wounds.[28] Onions also have a place in folklore and superstition. Ammi tells me that keeping an onion and a knife under your pillow at night helps fight off bad dreams.

One of the most commonly grown vegetables in our part of Asia, onions make the base for most gravies. In Bihar and Jharkhand, onions are eaten raw with roti and pickles. When I was in Madhya Pradesh for work and meeting farmers, they'd often have bajra roti or khichdi with onion. One of the farmers told me that this was a convenient meal because it is easy to pack and take to the field.

In restaurants, raw onions get a little makeover before they are served to patrons. Chefs slice them into circles and serve them topped with Kashmiri chilli, chaat masala, or just with lemon and salt. Smaller onions get soaked in vinegar, making the famous 'sirke wali pyaaz' (pickled onion), which can be served as an accompaniment to any dish. The most common Indian salad cannot be served without cucumber, tomato, carrots and, of course, onions. Raw onions also go well with kebabs; Shabi never eats kebabs without them. It is the only time I've seen him make an extra effort in the kitchen.

In the hostel, I always tried to avoid the task of chopping onions because it made me cry, but now as a chef I have no option – there is no Arshad or Moin to pass this job off to any more.

Even though I have not met Ashraf and the others in almost seven years, I've made his brilliant mutton curry often. The only difference between Ashraf's recipe and mine is that I marinate the meat overnight. In college, we never had the luxury or the patience to wait a whole night before we actually began eating. We were young and hungry. We always used a pressure cooker to cook the meat. Today, I take my time making this dish, leaving the spices in the meat to absorb overnight and slow-cooking it to give it a luxurious texture. But I hope to meet Ashraf soon so I can sit down with him to roll the chapatis and cook him this dish. It was our mutual love for food that brought us together in hostel, and it will be a delight to cook for him once again.

5. Add red chilli, coriander and cumin powder and mix well.
6. Add the fried onion paste and cook again. Add as much water as you'd like for the thickness of the gravy to be.
7. Adjust salt and spice.
8. Add the garam masala and cook on a low flame till the meat becomes tender and it falls off the bone.
9. Sprinkle some freshly chopped coriander and serve hot with tandoori naan.

## Recipe

Serves: 2

Cooking time: 90 minutes

### Ingredients

- ¼ cup ghee or oil
- 6–7 green cardamoms
- 1-inch cinnamon stick
- 2 bay leaves
- ½ tbsp ginger paste
- ½ tbsp garlic paste
- 500 gm mutton shanks
- 200 gm plain curd, beaten
- 2 tbsp red chilli powder
- 1 tbsp coriander powder
- 1 tbsp cumin powder
- 1 cup fried onion paste
- 1 tsp garam masala powder
- Salt to taste
- ¼ bunch fresh coriander finely chopped

### Method

1. Heat ghee/oil in a deep pan.
2. Add cardamom, cinnamon and bay leaves. Let it sp then add ginger–garlic paste and cook for 2–3 minu
3. Toss in the mutton shanks and cook over a high fla 8–10 minutes till it turns brown.
4. Reduce the flame to medium heat and add beaten cur it gently and ensure that it coats the mutton pieces Cook till the oil separates.

# 13

# Haleem

ONCE, ON A BLISSFULLY peaceful Thursday evening, I remember a highly excited Ashraf calling me for a food jaunt. 'Come now,' he commanded, 'to Hotel Nigar. There is haleem.' Since I had never eaten haleem before (it's odd that it was never made at a food lover's home like mine), a few friends and I quickly dressed and walked the 500 metres to the small joint where Ashraf was already seated. In minutes we were served plates of haleem topped with fresh coriander, chillies, fried onions and lemon wedges, all for a princely sum of ₹15. It was a hearty meal, one that I was rather satisfied with. However, I had no idea that it would one day become part of my top-five favourite Muslim dishes. And like its name, an Arabic word which means 'patient', I would have to wait to come to that realization, which makes sense since this is a slow-cooked dish.

Haleem is a porridge-like dish, bursting with flavour. But its tricky, labour-intensive technique has endangered it. It demands long hours to cook and isn't feasible with our modern lifestyles or cooking implements. And so, haleem has almost disappeared from the plates of most families too. One can easily find haleem in Hyderabad, but in cities like Delhi or Mumbai, one has to seek it out, perhaps in the older parts of town where this age-old tradition of cooking has continued.

The origins of haleem are sketchy. Some say it is traditionally a Shia Muslim dish, which came from Persia and was consumed to commemorate the martyrdom of Imam Hussain (may Allah be pleased with him), the grandson of Prophet Muhammad (peace be upon him), during Muharram and Ramzan. Alan Davidson, in *The Oxford Companion to Food,* writes that haleem is an important and unusual dish, popular in Iran, Afghanistan and India; it is known as harissa in Turkey and the eastern Arab world. He further quotes Magaret Shaida, author of *The Legendary Cuisine of Persia,* who states that this dish was invented by the sixth-century Persian King Khosrow and that when Muslims conquered Persia a century later, it became a firm favourite of the Prophet. Its fame and the popularity were thus assured, and it spread all over the Middle East.[29, 30]

Annia Ciezadlo, in her article 'History on a Plate' writes that the first written recipe for harissa dates back to the tenth century, when a scribe named Ibn Sayyar al-Warraq compiled a book of dishes favoured by the Caliphs of Islam's so-called Golden Age. The recipe for harissa in his *Kitab al-Tabikh* (Book of Dishes) – the world's oldest surviving Arabic cookbook (published in the tenth century) – is strikigly similar to the one people in the Middle East eat to this day.[31]

It is not hard to imagine that this hearty, nutrient-rich, one-pot meal travelled to India with sailors and Arab soldiers through their arduous journey, just the way we, when travelling abroad, take with us a little khakra, achaar, laddu, etc., to remind us of the flavours of home. And as it travelled, the dish itself evolved, absorbing the spices of the lands it passed, to transform into something much more exciting and flavourful than its prototype. Bisma Tarmizi writes that haleem, nihari and biryani were robustly rustic dishes before they were refined and polished for the tables of royalty in the Subcontinent. These hearty dishes were seen as cantonment foods and meant to feed the '*lashkaray fauj*' (army battalions). It was a complete dish for sailors and soldiers, and that is how some historians believe harissa came to the coast of Malabar with the arrival of Arab traders.[32]

Dr Pushpesh Pant, food critic and historian, describes this dish perfectly, saying, 'Haleem is prepared with *char ghaf* – *gehu, gosht*, ghee, *gur* [four Gs – wheat, meat, ghee and jaggery]. The gur is the typically Hyderabadi addition. They like their food sweet and sour.'[33] The basic principle of all harissa, haleem or khichda (another popular Muslim dish) is the same – wheat and meat should be in a 1:2 ratio. Harissa is a simple and (as per the Indian palate) rather bland dish made with just meat, wheat, cinnamon and ghee.

I fell in love with haleem in Hyderabad. Once you've eaten this dish there, it ruins haleem for you anywhere else. Nothing compares to the stuff that Hyderabad offers because it includes the right amount of spices, is perfectly creamy and has the right texture. Haleem in Hyderabad is often spicier than its counterparts elsewhere in the country.

Today I've tasted haleem in many places, even as part of a tasting menu at a restaurant in New Delhi. In fact, these days, there is also a chicken haleem available in the market for those who don't like red meat, and I have also heard of vegetarian haleem, which, quite frankly, is blasphemy. Last year during Ramzan I was in Bengaluru to run a workshop, and I wanted to show off my culinary skills to my old friend Manasi, who was travelling with me. She has no standards when it comes to food, in fact, she often prefers burnt food to perfectly cooked dishes, so impressing her is not difficult. It was a pleasant evening and we found ourselves at a busy food street near the hotel we were staying at. Ambling along, we soon came across a cart selling luqmi (keema samosas) and haleem. Manasi had never eaten either before so we decided to give it a try. Even though they claimed it was Hyderabadi haleem, I found it bland and dry. I was disappointed that her first experience of a dish I loved so much was unsatisfactory and not representative of 'true' haleem. But I can understand why so many places get it wrong. This is a difficult dish to replicate; most people end up over-spicing it when, in fact, haleem asks only for garam masala and cumin, and not many other spices. The consistency too is key. Haleem should be like porridge, not a paste and not runny either.

Even though haleem was never made at home, there was, apparently, a master of the dish in the family. My father told me that my late aunt, Surraiya Aunty's, haleem was simply unparalleled. Unfortunately, I had never had the chance to eat food cooked by her. I've often wanted to make haleem for my parents, but when it comes to food, they're my biggest critics. And given how hard they're to please in the first place, a complicated dish like haleem isn't ideal. But one day, a few days before Ramzan, I summoned up the courage to do it. You'll never know till you try, right?

I bought mutton from Hauz Rani market, in Malviya Nagar, Delhi. The market is always busy with people buying meat, shopping for groceries and tenants roaming the streets. There are quite a few meat shops in Malviya Nagar, but there's a specific shop I go to; they know I cook often and that I am picky about the meat I buy. When buying mutton for haleem, one should always get boneless meat, especially from the fattier and juicier hind thighs of the animal. One should also avoid the chops and bones. The meat has to melt with the other grains and lentils; so it is important to buy meat with minimal bones and maximum flavour. I also ask the butcher to cut the meat pieces as small as possible and get some extra fat thrown in, which will add richness to the dish.

Back home, I washed the meat thoroughly and set it aside while I prepared the kitchen. People often use a pressure cooker to cook haleem quickly, but I feel that it kills all the flavour of the meat. It's better to use a deep vessel to boil the meat, lentils and wheat. Once the meat and grains were cooked and boiled properly, I blended them in the mixer – not a common practice in stand-alone haleem restaurants. I cooked this mixture on a low flame for four to five hours, and then, using a big wooden spatula, I mixed all of it together so that the meat and lentils became a thick paste.

After two-and-a-half hours of intense effort, my dish was ready. I topped it with fried onions, fresh coriander and chopped green chillies, with a sprinkling of extra cumin and lemon wedges on the side, just the way I had had it in Hotel Nigar in Ranchi the first time. As they say, the proof of the pudding is in the eating, and my parents loved it, even expressing surprise that it turned out so well on my first try. I'm not quite near the Hyderabadi standard of haleem yet, but one should always have a standard to aspire to and that is mine.

## Recipe

Serves: 8 to 10
Cooking time: 120 to 150 minutes (soaking time separate)

### Ingredients

- 1 cup broken wheat
- ½ cup channa dal

- ¼ cup urad dal
- ¼ cup moong dal
- ¼ cup masoor dal
- ¼ cup basmati rice
- ¼ cup barley
- ¾ cup ghee
- 2 large onions (sliced for frying)
- 3 tbsp ginger–garlic paste
- 2 kg mutton, boneless
- 1 tsp turmeric powder
- 1 tbsp red chilli powder
- 1 tbsp coriander powder
- 2 cups mutton stock or water
- Salt to taste
- 2–3 green chillies, chopped
- 1 tsp garam masala powder
- ¼ tsp nutmeg powder
- ¼ tsp mace powder
- ½ tsp black cumin
- ½ tsp green cardamom powder

## Method

1. Wash and rinse all the grains and soak it for at least six hours or overnight.
2. In a deep pan, pour some ghee and fry the onions until brown and crispy.
3. Add ginger–garlic paste and sauté for 2–3 minutes or till the rawness goes away.
4. Toss in the meat, chillies, turmeric, chilli powder, coriander powder, stock/water and salt. Cook until the meat is cooked and fork-tender.

5. In another pot, boil all the pre-soaked grains in ample water. You can adjust the water based on the consistency you'd like. This should take 2–3 hours or, to save time, use a pressure cooker and remove after 5–6 whistles.
6. Once boiled, blend the grains in a grinder into a pouring paste, and then put it back in the pot.
7. Once cooled, make a paste of the meat using either a mixer grinder or a heavy spatula.
8. Mix the meat into the pot of grain and lower the flame. Let it cook for 8–10 minutes.
9. Adjust the seasoning.
10. Dry roast garam masala, nutmeg, mace, black cumin and green cardamom. Make a smooth powder and sprinkle this into the meat. Mix it well, cover with a lid and let the haleem cook on a very low flame for 10–12 more minutes.

# 14

# Mansa Jhola

NICKNAMES ARE A DANGEROUS thing. Once they are attached, they usually stick around for life. One of my friends in college, Shakeel, once made the mistake of showing us a picture of himself of which he was very proud. In the photograph, Shakeel sports a haircut similar to Salman Khan's in the film *Tere Naam*. He thought he looked smashing, and fancied it was the best photograph of himself. But of course, it was far from the truth. He looked funny, but Shakeel lived under the illusion that he looked his best in that picture. And this earned him the nickname Radhe, after Salman Khan's character in the movie, because of his stupidity.

Shakeel lived alone in Ranchi, in a small room, which cost him just ₹200 a month. The floor was uneven, there were uncemented patches on the roof and posters covered the walls. Poetry books and Urdu works were strewn everywhere, and the scent of sandalwood incense hung in the air – a habit I would pick up from him. Shakeel wasn't from a well-off family, and he had to make do with whatever little money his parents could send him.

Despite the lack of space, Shakeel had managed to clear out a small kitchen in one corner of the room, under a window. He loved food, but there was one major problem – he had never set foot in the kitchen while he had been home in Odisha. But since he was now on his own, he had to learn. His mother had taught him a few basic dishes, which he cooked in rotation.

It was the week before our semester examinations, and a few friends and I had made plans to study together. We took the narrow staircase up to Shakeel's on the third floor and parked ourselves wherever we could find place. In my experience, people do everything but study when they meet in a study group – and that was just what happened. At around 8 p.m., our host got up to cook us some food and we promised ourselves that we would study after dinner, even though, deep down, we knew that wasn't going to happen, at least not that day. Shakeel was making a simple mutton curry his mother had taught him. He called it 'mansa jhola'.

While Shakeel was cooking the mutton, I soaked the rice in a pot that was usually used to boil milk. Someone started playing popular local Jharkhandi songs, which none of us could understand, and that gave us another chance to make fun of each other, laughing at our terrible choice in music, and most importantly, endlessly mocking Shakeel's *Tere Naam* hairstyle. Soon the food was ready, and we helped ourselves to it.

I was astonished by this no-frills mutton curry. It had a heavy, aromatic flavour because of the whole spices, the onion and garlic gravy. The mutton was tender, and the potatoes absorbed all the flavours of the gravy. The dish was balanced without a single ingredient overpowering it.

Many years later, in 2015, I was travelling to Odisha, and I remembered that evening we had spent at Shakeel's house. I visited Kaipadar, 40 kilometres from Bhubaneshwar – home to the Siddha Purush Bokhari Baba's shrine, a unique place where people from different religions and cultures come to seek the blessings of Satyapir. It is believed that Satyapir derived his name from the Hindu god 'Satyanarayan' and the Islamic 'Peera'. Here, the confluence of Hindu and Muslim elements combine to create an interesting experience. In Islam, music is usually not allowed at a shrine, but here, while offering the *shirni*, a big drum-like instrument (bada katha) is beaten to celebrate. This element is borrowed from Hinduism, and specifically from the Bengalis, who use drums during their prayer rituals. Devotees who visit this shrine believe that their wishes will come true if they write it on a piece of a paper and hang it in the shrine.

Dr Manas Kumar Das, in his paper 'History of Odisha (from 1435 to 1803 AD)', argues that the Afghan rule in Odisha established a new Muslim era in the region's medieval history. The invasion of Sultan Sulaiman Karrani's son, Bayazid, and General Kalapahada in 1568 CE established Muslim rule over Odisha for the first time under the Afghans and then under the Mughals. He further states that more than 2,000 words of the Islamic languages entered into Odia literature.[34] I believe the language and the culture impacted the eating habits of the land; the consumption of red meat is one example.

While I was travelling around the city, I realized that the food preparation and the level of spice changes drastically from places that border Kolkata and those around Andhra Pradesh. I found many similarities between the food of Bengal and Odisha, but I have been told that as an expert, I shouldn't say this because of the nuances of both cuisines.

Suhail Akhtar, a journalist and friend, who grew up in Odisha, told me more about the mixed culture of Odisha – those who are not Odia prefer Bihari food, while others, especially those from Cuttack, love Odia food. People in Odisha eat fish and meat, and the preparation across groups is also similar. In areas closer to Andhra Pradesh, the food will be spicier than in other regions.

I had the opportunity to eat mansa jhola once again, and found it just as simple and delicious as Shakeel's. The spices used in the dish are found in the Bengali kosha mangsho and in ahuna (khada masala mutton) of Bihar. It is home-made comfort food, not found in restaurants.

In Delhi and other big cities, it is difficult to find Odia food. It is strange that even though Odia cooks are said to be one of the best in the country, and it is very common to find them working in restaurant kitchens, their food isn't as popular as that of its neighbouring states. Vikram Doctor, in his article 'India's Food Politics and How it Was Capable of Caste Promotion', quotes Arjun Appadurai and says, perhaps, it is because the food from the neighbouring states were being aggressively pushed: 'Telugu food is being progressively pushed out of sight by Tamil cuisine, Oriya by Bengali cuisine, Kannada by Marathi, Rajasthani by Gujarati, and Kashmiri by Punjabi.'[35]

That day, in Shakeel's room, we shared a meal and created a memory. For me, mansa jhola will always bring back warm memories of my simple and uncomplicated youth, and the days we spent in Shakeel's small room, our laughter echoing, the jokes and friendly ribbing as we sat around pretending to study, while the rice bubbled in the milk pan and the smell of spices filled the room, snuffing out the heady scent of sandalwood. Mansa jhola is a dish that makes me believe in the simple yet powerful value of our core ingredients. Often, to enjoy something delicious and wonderful, you don't need expensive ingredients; the answers lie in the humble and simple offerings in your kitchen.

## Recipe

Serves: 3 to 4

Cooking time: 80 to 90 minutes (marination time separate)

### Ingredients

- ½ kg mutton
- 2-inch cinnamon sticks
- 6 green cardamoms
- 4 cloves
- 1 tsp black pepper
- 5 medium onions
- 3-inch ginger
- 10–12 garlic cloves
- 2 tbsp mustard oil
- 2 bay leaves
- 2 dry red chillies
- 2 medium potatoes, chopped into halves
- 2 tsp turmeric powder
- 2 tsp meat masala powder
- 2 tsp red chilli powder
- Salt to taste

### Method

1. Marinate the meat in turmeric powder and salt for 120 minutes.
2. In a pan, dry roast cinnamon, cardamom, cloves and black pepper till they release their aroma. Grind the spices into a fine powder.
3. Using a blender, make a paste out of the onions, ginger and garlic.

4. In a pressure cooker, heat the mustard oil on a high flame till it smokes.
5. Throw in the bay leaves with one sliced onion and the red chillies. Sauté till the onions turn golden brown.
6. Add the onion and ginger–garlic paste. Top it up with turmeric powder and chilli powder. Cook over a medium flame for 5–7 minutes.
7. Add the marinated mutton and potatoes. Ensure the potatoes are cut in two halves only.
8. Sauté for 10 minutes or till the meat turns brown. Add about 3 cups of water.
9. Add the meat masala powder and salt.
10. Put on the lid and let it cook for 15–20 minutes over a medium flame.
11. Switch off the flame and let it sit till the air from the pressure cooker releases.
12. Serve hot with rice.

# 15

# *Dal Dunghar*

AFTER GRADUATING FROM COLLEGE, I came back home to Ramgarh. Most of my college friends had left for Delhi or other big cities in search of jobs or to study further. I would often speak to them regarding their whereabouts and the lives they were leading. I also spent a lot of time talking to Abbi about things I might want to do in the future, how I could earn a living and create a better life for myself. 'Why don't you also pack your bags and go to Delhi? You have some work experience and your brother already works there. Go do something interesting,' Abbi would say to me. I wasn't ready to leave home yet, but I knew I had to do something and that my father's advice was wise. So, one morning, I asked Abbi to buy me a one-way ticket to Delhi.

Once the date for my departure was fixed, the enormity of my decision struck me. I was going to leave a space I had spent 20 years of my life in. Everything was coming to a swift end. I slept in my small room, committing every corner to memory, noticing the patches and marks on the walls I had never seen before. I spent many sleepless nights listening to music, reliving memories of school, college, my first job at the print media house, my friends, my red cycle, my kabbadi and volleyball teams, and the other little experiences that had made up my life so far.

Finally, the day arrived when I was supposed to bid farewell to everything and every connection I had with Ramgarh. As always, Ammi had packed food for the journey, and as she handed it to me, I could see her eyes were damp. She must have been confident that I would make something of myself in Delhi, but my going away also broke her heart. Abbi dropped me to the railway station on his bike – I didn't have much luggage – and bid me good luck. He hugged me tightly and said, 'Allah hafiz (May God be with you).'

Early the next morning I was at New Delhi Railway Station with a bag full of clothes and a heart heavy with memories. It was only when I saw Shabi waiting on the platform, waving his hands and calling out to me, that I felt at ease. I drew courage from his familiar smile. 'Welcome to Dilli,' he said. 'This place is completely different from what you're used to, but the city will win you over. Let's go home.'

We took an auto to Shabi's flat in Khirki Extension. To entertain me, Shabi kept pointing out all the landmarks on our way. I plastered a smile on my face, but inside I was split between two contradictory emotions – my heart sinking at the thought of what I'd left behind, the chapter of my life that was closing. And yet, it was also rising at the thought of the new beginning that was awaiting me. Forty-five minutes later we arrived at our destination. The small lanes that we crossed were either damp or waterlogged, around the corner there were a few street vendors selling samosas or pani puri, a juice shop and a few other stores. This seemed just like any other lane in Ramgarh and it offered me a sense of familiarity. Once I freshened up, Shabi fed me a meal of freshly made roti, a baingan sabzi (brinjal dish) and dal from the night before. The baingan was cooked in a tangy gravy, but it was the dal that caught my attention. This was partially because

I don't like baingan (Ammi always said that baingan is *bey-gun,* a vegetable with no quality). I can tolerate baingan when it is cooked in the Bengali-style baingan bhaja (fried in mustard oil) or as baingan bhartha.

Creamy and smoky, the dal was unique. Even later, as the two of us sat watching TV, my focus remained on the dal. What was the flavour and why was it smoky? I'd never tasted anything like it before. The next morning, I asked Shabi where exactly he'd ordered the dal from, and he told me it was from a place called Zaika 55 – fifty-five for the number of dishes they served. I was excited at the prospect of eating more of it.

Zaika 55 turned out to be a small shop. At the counter in front sat a young man, taking orders and collecting cash. Behind him, there was a small sticker which said 'Allah and Mohammed' written in Arabic. I flipped through the menu, clueless about the name of the dal I was looking for. The owner's name was Naseem Mushtaq, and when I enquired about the smoky dal I had had a few days ago, he smiled and pointed out the 'Zaika special dal' on the menu. It turned out that Naseem's special dal was one of the most ordered dishes, especially with garlic butter naan. He told me that it wasn't a difficult dish to make; what it required was an exact measurement of rajma (kidney beans), kali dal (black lentils) and moong dal with the correct ratio of onions and tomatoes. But the most crucial element was how much time it took to smoke the dish. Smoking it too long would make it bitter and unappetizing, whereas smoking it for the exact time could do wonders. I thanked him for his advice; it was refreshing to find a restaurant owner sharing their recipes, which usually are their most guarded secrets. Armed with his special recipe, and a pot of dal with garlic naan, I left his shop happy to have made a connection with Naseem Bhai.

Smoking a dish is called '*dunghar dena*' – a unique way of adding smoke to any dish. In this method, hot charcoal is put in a heatproof or metal bowl and drizzled with ghee. This bowl is then placed in a cooked dish (in this case, it was the dal) and it is covered with a lid so that the smoke gets locked in and is absorbed by the ingredients. One can use whole spices like cinnamon sticks, cloves or any other spice to flavour the smoke. This simple method can elevate a simple home-cooked dal to gourmet standards in seconds.

Lentils have been a staple in Indian cuisine since the Indus Valley Civilization. According to Madhulika Dash, dal finds mention in ancient scriptures such as the *Manasollasa,* and in epics such as the Mahabharata. A special kind of channa dal was prepared to mark Chandragupta Maurya's marriage to Princess Helena in 303 BCE.[36] Sanchari Pal writes in her article, 'Food Fit for Royalty', that in medieval India it was the revival of the dum pukht technique (slow-cooking in steam) that raised the stature of dal, especially channa dal (Bengal gram), in royal menus. Channa dal was a favourite of the Mughals; they liked the dal's creamy texture. In fact, the khansamas were under orders to specifically serve only this form of lentils. A popular story is that Shah Jahan's son Murad Baksh preferred moong dal, and he ate it with a tadka of ghee, chaat masala and freshly chopped coriander and onion (Abbi, like Murad Baksh, also enjoyed his dal with ghee). This preparation is now famously known as 'Moradabadi dal'. A little smoked ghee with caramelized onions goes a long way in transforming a dish from good to great.

My first meal in Delhi got me excited about the food journey that awaited me here. This new dal held the promise of more exciting discoveries ahead. Little did I know then that it would be surprises like this that would one day catapult me into a full-blown culinary adventure that would involve starting my own venture, a pop-up café, an exciting stint on MasterChef, working with a few cafés and restaurants, my blog, and ultimately, this book.

---

## Recipe

Serves: 4
Cooking time: 45 minutes

### Ingredients

- ¼ cup moong dal (split moong beans)
- ¼ cup tuvar dal (split pigeon pea)
- ¼ cup channa dal (split chickpeas)
- 1 tsp salt
- ¼ tsp turmeric powder
- 3¼ cup water
- 1 small onion, chopped
- 1 small tomato, chopped
- ¼ tsp mustard seeds
- ½ tsp cumin seeds
- 2 pieces dried red chillies
- A pinch of hing (asafoetida)
- ½ tsp coriander powder
- ½ tsp garam masala powder
- 2 tsp kasuri methi
- 1 tsp chopped coriander leaves
- 3 tbsp ghee
- 2 pieces of charcoal
- ¼ cup fried onion

## Method

1. Wash, clean, drain and dry all the dals.
2. In a pressure cooker, heat some ghee and roast all the dals till they turn slightly brown.
3. Add salt, turmeric and water. Close the lid and pressure cook for 4 whistles. Open the cooker once all the pressure is released.
4. In another pan, heat ghee and add cumin, mustard seeds, chillies and hing till it splutters.
5. Toss in the chopped onions and tomatoes and sauté till they become soft and tender.
6. Add this tadka to the dal along with coriander powder, garam masala and kasuri methi.
7. Bring to a boil then reduce the flame and cook for 5 minutes. Adjust the consistency of dal by adding water.
8. Light up the charcoal and place it in a steel bowl. Put this steel bowl in the pressure cooker and pour ghee on the charcoal. Cover the lid and let it smoke for 8–10 minutes.
9. Take the lid off and mix freshly chopped coriander and fried onion.
10. Eat with butter roti or naan.

# 16

# Aslam's Butter Chicken

THE POET MIR TAQI MIR once described the city of Delhi as, '*Koochey nahin Dilli ke, auraaq-e-musawwir hain/Jo shakl nazar aayi, tasveer nazar aayi* (These are not Delhi by-lanes, these are an artist's canvas/Every sight I see looks like a painting).' If there is a place that brings these lines to life, it is Purani Dilli, or Old Delhi as it is now known. Here, there is beauty in chaos and one can even find peace amidst the endless honking. There are two lives in Old Delhi: *ek shab aur dusra sehar* (one in the morning and the other in the evening). In the morning, the place is bustling with people at work selling, buying, eating, cooking; but the evenings are different. The pace slows down, a sense of calm pervades the neighbourhood, people wrap up their work and head to *kebabchi*s (expert kebab-makers) for some food and *gupshup* (chit-chat). I love going to Purani Dilli to indulge in the food and take lots of photographs. Old Delhi, popular as it is for its chai, korma and kebabs, is also home to a very unusual butter chicken.

I had eaten this delicious, creamy delicacy everywhere – at Moti Mahal, the Daryaganj institution, Dhaba by the Claridges, at popular food joints in Amritsar and Ludhiana, and at Goila's Butter Chicken, Chef Saransh Goila's restaurant in Mumbai. Any Indian restaurant menu will be incomplete without this dish. So, when a colleague told me that I had to try Aslam's butter chicken in Old Delhi, I scoffed at the idea. How could it be any different from what I had already tried?

Then one day, while pottering around Old Delhi taking photos, I stumbled upon a three-storey building a little ahead of Karim's with a sign for Aslam's Butter Chicken. Marinated chicken hung on skewers next to the charcoal grills and the tangy smell was inviting and made my mouth water. The crowd outside the joint quickly dispersed any doubts I had.

The pace inside was maddening; cooks and servers working relentlessly, customers thronging the counter, shouting to get their orders noticed and processed. Surprised and curious at the enthusiasm for a common fare like butter chicken, I joined the crowd and ordered a plate. I noticed they also had chicken seekh, fish and paneer on the menu, but the crowd was here for the butter chicken – the star of the show. And then I realized the reason for its popularity – the ladles of melted butter spooned on to the meat. The charcoal grill at Aslam's was used not just to cook the chicken but also melt butter in an old, rustic deep pan. Melting butter on a flame gives it a lovely smoky and nutty flavour. This was poured on to the chicken, making it moist and juicy. This was not just any butter chicken, it was an ultra-deluxe version of the dish.

The prodigious quantities of butter being used took me back to Manek Chowk in Ahmedabad, a jewellery market that transforms into a food paradise in the evenings. I was there for a workshop, and when I was done I took a stroll around. What I witnessed was shocking. Imagine one plate of pao bhaji or dosa with more than 100 grams of butter or sandwiches with all sorts of stuffing, topped with layers and layers of grated cheese and, of course, more butter. I ate a chocolate sandwich that had layers of melted chocolate, chocolate chips, pineapple jam, lots of grated cheese, dollops of butter, and ice-cream sandwiched between four slices of bread, grilled and served with an extra topping of cheese, butter and melted chocolate! Absolutely delicious, and sinful. I couldn't finish it on my own.

At Aslam's Butter Chicken, I was served the dish in a steel container with a basket of roomali roti. The perfectly cooked and chargrilled pieces of chicken were swimming in a pool of butter and spices. Aslam's twist on this classic dish was the use of curd, cream and lots of butter as its base, instead of the usual tomato, cream and butter. The gravy was salty with the tang of chaat masala, and the generous cream and curd cut the spice level, simultaneously cooling the stomach. The chicken, too, was flavoured with at least 20 different spices, making it unique and giving it an edge usually not found at other restaurants. They say the classic butter chicken goes best with plain or garlic naan, but roomali roti complemented Aslam's version better. I ate the dish while taking in the chaotic view of Old Delhi. Rickshaws choked the narrow lanes, people bustled about carrying bags of goods and produce on their backs, and every once in a while there'd be a curious passer-by, camera in hand, gazing at the beauty of Old Delhi. Most people end up going to the same old tried and tested (and iconic) places like Karim's, Al Jawahar, Kuremal Mohan Lal Kulfi Wale or eating snacks like chole kulche, chaat or the parathas in Old Delhi, and often we miss out on the lesser-known gems of the city. I left with a promise to come back to Aslam's to dig out its history.

There are many stories about how butter chicken came to be, and as usual, a good-old conflict about its exact origin. The commonly accepted story is that butter chicken was invented in the Moti Mahal kitchens in Daryaganj, Old Delhi, and that the man behind the creation was Kundan Lal Gujral. After Partition,

Kundan moved to Delhi from Peshawar. He set up a shop in Daryaganj, cooking and serving the recipes from his hometown. He used a tandoor to cook food, thus creating the first-ever tandoori chicken this side of the border. He was an inspiration for many people, who started using tandoors to cook their food. It was not long before Gujral realized that tandoori chicken tends to dry up if left out too long, and so he added a gravy of tomatoes, butter and cream to the chicken and brought forth into the world the butter chicken we all know and love.

The other conflicting story comes from a faraway land. According to Britannica, butter chicken was invented in the 1970s by a Bangladeshi chef in Glasgow, Scotland. The chef had added a mild tomato-cream sauce to his chicken tikka to make it more palatable for the Western palate.[37] I don't know which story is real, but I do prefer the Moti Mahal story.

During Ramzan, as part of my usual pilgrimage to the food joints in Old Delhi, I revisited Aslam's. I reached Old Delhi prepared with my camera and an empty stomach, ready to fill it up with butter chicken. Aslam, the owner, is a broad-shouldered, mustachioed man. He wore a green cap and a tight T-shirt that hugged his belly – proving that he was a food lover. His father had opened the shop in 1988, and the unique spice mix for his chicken tikka that everyone was crazy about was invented by his grandfather. Aslam's had started out as a one-table and grill restaurant, but soon gained a cult following. When asked about the 20 spices used in the chicken, he declined to answer. He didn't reveal his secret spice mix but did give me some marinated meat to take home.

There are many copycat versions of Aslam's butter chicken – a testament to its popularity – however none come close to the original. And the secret probably lies in the carefully guarded spice mix recipe. In fact, Aslam adds the spice mix into the meat himself, lest anyone learn its secret.

In an era where almost all Indian gravies taste similar because of the ubiquitous tomato, onion and ginger–garlic base, Aslam's butter chicken is a relief. Yes, their dish is full of butter and calories, and possibly hell for those who are calorie conscious, but I believe one can spare a day every few months to indulge in this sinful preparation. It's worth knowing why so many people wait patiently in queue to get their fix.

The recipe that I am sharing is definitely not the original, but it's as close to the original as I could decipher from what I ate. The recreation is possible by the addition of green chilli paste and the kaala chaat masala you can find in either Kinari Bazaar or Khari Baoli of Old Delhi. The butter chicken should always be eaten hot and on the same day, otherwise the butter will coagulate and destroy the flavour. This recipe is my attempt to bring Aslam's famous offering into your homes.

## Recipe

Serves: 4
Cooking time: 120 to 140 minutes

### Ingredients

- 1 kg chicken
- 2 tbsp onion paste (1 large onion will make the paste)
- 2 tbsp ginger–garlic paste
- 1 tbsp green chilli paste
- 3 tbsp hung curd
- Salt to taste

- 8 tbsp melted butter
- 3 tsp chaat masala
- 1 tsp garam masala
- 2 tbsp cumin powder
- 1 piece charcoal
- 2 tbsp ghee
- 100 gm + 100 gm cream and curd
- Freshly chopped coriander and lemon juice to garnish

## Method

1. Marinate the chicken in onion, ginger–garlic and green chilli paste, along with the hung curd, salt, 2 tablespoons of melted butter, chaat masala, garam masala and cumin powder. Let it sit for 90 minutes.
2. To give the chicken a smoky flavour, light up the charcoal and put it in a small steel bowl. Place this in the centre of the bowl in which the chicken is being marinated. Pour some ghee on the charcoal and close the bowl's lid. Let it sit for 5–8 minutes, then remove the lid.
3. Skewer the chicken pieces on to the metal or wooden skewers and place them on a grilling pan. For the best results, use an open flame griller or an electric griller.
4. Grill for 8–10 minutes. Keep brushing the ghee on the meat to keep it moist through the process.
5. Once the chicken pieces are well-cooked, remove them from the skewers and place them in a bowl.
6. Add 6 tablespoons of butter, the cream and curd mix and chaat masala powder into the same bowl as the chicken. Toss properly.
7. Garnish with freshly chopped coriander and lemon juice. Serve hot with roomali roti.

# 17

# Mirchi ka Salan

THERE ARE MANY PERKS of living in Delhi, including exciting food tours and heritage walks. I have been on many food tours across the city, my favourite still being those that take me to Old Delhi, which I think is the heart of cultural and historical Delhi. Some of the popular food establishments these walks cover are places like Karim's, Al Jawahar, Kuremal Mohan Lal Kulfiwale, with a taste of unique dishes such as dhaga kebab and butter coffee. I always find a reason to visit Old Delhi, sometimes heading there at least four or five times a month, either to eat, to explore its narrow lanes or to just take pictures.

On one food walk through Old Delhi that I was part of, I met Bilal Saleem. A bespectacled, tall, clean-shaven man with thick, black curly hair, Bilal Saleem had a deep, husky voice and was surprisingly soft-spoken. It was his manner of speech, in fact, that caught my attention. Curious and friendly, he approached me and soon our conversation effortlessly veered to the subject of food. It was a pleasant coincidence that Bilal also lived in Khirki, a few houses away from mine, and so, once we were done with our walk, we took a taxi back home together. On our way, he told me about his childhood in Hyderabad, how listening to stories from his elders and maulanas had sparked in him a passion for storytelling as an art form. Through his stories Bilal wanted to touch people's souls, he wanted to make *ek ruhani tallukat* (a soulful connection), and hence he came to Delhi and began working in theatre. He invited me to his house for a meal, telling me that his ammi made the best biryani and mirchi ka salan (Bilal had clearly never met my mother, because when it comes to biryani, no one can beat Ammi). I accepted his offer; we were to meet the following week.

The next week, I navigated the alleys of Khirki, passing the small tea shops and the tucked-away Muslim restaurants with their enticing aroma of kebabs, nihari and khamiri roti. Evenings in Khirki Extention are a world unto themselves. Small pakora and chai stalls mushroom and soon draw a crowd, where discussions about politics, movies or their daily lives take place over cup after cup of hot tea. These are scenes that are quickly dying with the gentrification of neighbourhoods.

Soon I arrived at Bilal's, a small, brightly lit home. It was *isha* namaz time (the last prayer of the day) and Bilal Bhai's mother, Nisar Aunty, was finishing her prayers. Bilal Bhai took me to the kitchen where he offered me a drink – Roohafza mixed with sugar and milk. I tend to ingratiate myself into people's kitchens to help, but Bilal Bhai was ready with everything and all that was left for me to do was sit around their dastarkhān and enjoy the food.

Once she was done with her namaz, Nisar Aunty served us a lavish feast of biryani, mirchi ka salan, burani raita, khus sherbet, salad and chane ka halwa. I was struck by her mirchi ka salan, a sweet and spicy offering bursting with flavour. '*Salna*' or '*salan*' is an Urdu word for curry. This mirchi ka salan was made of green chillies, peanuts, sesame seeds, dry coconut, cumin seeds, ginger and garlic paste, turmeric powder, bay leaves and thick tamarind juice. It enjoys the status of being a famous Hyderabadi delicacy, usually accompanied with Hyderbadi kachay gosht ki biryani or dum ki biryani. I asked her when she'd first learned to cook, to which she replied that she couldn't even remember. She loved making biryani for her kids, and living in Hyderabad had given her access to really aromatic spices from across the state.

Technique plays a big role in Hyderabadi cuisine, and mirchi ka salan is one such example. It employs a complex method, which, when done right, allows one to retain the texture of green chillies within a creamy, rich gravy. The primary goal is to keep the chillies intact and not break them during the cooking process. Another unique aspect of Hyderabadi cuisine is the use of tamarind, which is not common in north India.

Salan is much like our ubiquitous curry, which itself has a long and vibrant history in India. Journalist Soity Banerjee has written extensively about the evidence of a 400-year-old 'proto curry', which was found at the height of the Indus Valley Civilization. The three key ingredients used in their cooking were ginger, garlic and turmeric. Anthropologists also found traces of curry and starch grains in human teeth and in a cooking pot in the ancient town of Farmana (currently known as Daksh Khera in Rohtak, Haryana).[38] Also, researchers and anthropologists Arunima Kashyap and Steve Weber date the discovery of curry to between 2500 BCE and 2200 BCE.[39]

Today mirchi ka salan is usually considered a side dish, but this wasn't always the case. Madhulika Dash suggests that mirchi ka salan was Akbar's favourite dish; he loved the flavour profile of this dish – spicy, tangy and creamy, all at once. According to Dash, the *Ain-i-Akbari* mentions that mirchi ka salan was one of the dishes served at Akbar's coronation ceremony as the emperor of India (in 1556). However, there is no mention that it was created during Akbar's reign and it is possible the dish originated in the Qutb Shahi dynasty in the 1500s.[40]

Aloo Salan

Ratalu Kachalu ki Chaat

Nizam's Chicken Kathi Roll

Murgh Musallam

Akhti

Paan

Ashraf's Fried Onion Mutton Curry

Haleem

Mansa Jhola

Ghosht Taar Korma

Khubani Malai Kofta

Bun Kebab

Gulzar Zaidi's Kat-a-Kat

Ummi Abdulla's Vendakka Mulakittathu

# 18

# Ghosht Taar Korma

THERE ARE MANY PEOPLE and situations one can avoid and say no to, but one's mother is not among them. So when Ammi coerced me into going to a distant cousin's birthday party, I couldn't get out of it. Shabi, on the other hand, always had his way and hence, did not come. The party was teeming with my aunts, many of whom I do not remember meeting before. Each one of them greeted me with quintessential aunty statements such as, '*Kitne bade ho gaye, beta*', and, '*Kya kar rahe ho aaj–kal?*' (You have grown up so much, son,' and 'What are you doing these days?) When the opportunity presented itself, I escaped to a quiet corner with some food and spent my time watching the kids running around, tripping and falling over each other. That's when I met Amna Khala.

Sixty-year-old Amna Khala had flaming red henna-dyed hair, which is quite common in the Muslim community, with a spirit to match. She was rattled because she had not enjoyed the food and was looking for someone to complain about it to. She knew about my interest in food and sought me out. Amna Khala began her rant: '*Ye bawarchi ko toh kuch nahi aata* (This cook doesn't know anything).' She added that there was no masala in the food. It turned out that Amna Khala had offered to cook for the party, but since it was a big gathering, they'd asked her to sit back and enjoy herself.

Amna Khala had came to Delhi when she was 19, after she got married, but her heart was still in Lucknow, where she'd grown up. 'Dilli *achhi hai lekin,* Lucknow *mein rooh basti hai* (Delhi is good, but my soul is in Lucknow),' she said. Like her parents, she wanted to be buried in Lucknow. It was surprising that she still associated so deeply with Lucknow, despite having lived most of her life in Delhi. Then she went on to talk about her husband's love for her food. Her eyes shone with pride. She did not believe in ordering or eating food from outside. Her logic was simple: if I can cook awesome food, why order in? I pressed her for her favourite delicacies, in case she mentioned something I'd never heard of before. She asked me if I had ever had Rampuri korma (also known as ghosht taar korma)? My ears perked up at the mention. I had never heard of this dish before. It was among her father's favourite dishes. He would eat half a kilo of it with tandoori naan, she said.

Rampur, Uttar Pradesh, is famous for many things: the poet Mirza Ghalib had once called the city his home, the famous Rampuri *chaku* (knives) and its unique cuisine. The cuisine is not Mughlai, Awadhi or Hyderabadi; it is distinctly its own. And the establishment of Rampur itself is what played a big role in it. The Rohilla kingdom of Rampur was born under British protection in 1774. Interestingly, this deal, struck between Nawab Faizullah Khan and the British, led to Rampur becoming one of the most culturally important areas in north India.

Shashank Angiras, in his article 'Eat like Royalty', records that after coming under British protection, Rampur became a safe haven for all sorts of artists, architects, writers and chefs. Many of these people had migrated to Rampur after the Revolt of 1857.

Some had come to find work, but many had come to escape spaces where they couldn't freely express their artistic talents. Famous names like Mirza Ghalib, after fleeing Delhi, received patronage from the Rampur court. But beyond these famous artists, scores of cooks and khansamas from other princely states also made Rampur their home. This confluence of cultures is one of the primary reasons why Rampur's food seems to have been influenced by various regions like Delhi, Lucknow, Hyderabad and Kashmir.[41] It was the migration of khansamas to this small town in 1858 that has given Rampuri food its unique flavour.

Recently, I attended the Rampur Food Festival in Gurugram. The event was curated by food writer and critic Osama Jalali, and he discussed at length the elements of Rampuri cuisine, which include the subtle and limited use of spice, the technique of disguising ingredients, and the invention of unique dishes like ghosht ka halwa, adrak halwa, laute palaute and aloo ka zarda, to name a few. I learned from him that it was in Rampur that papaya was first used as a meat tenderizer, and this was also where gold and silver varq was first added to food.

According to Madhulika Dash, during the culinary renaissance in Rampur, there were so many chefs in the city that each one could focus on creating their own dishes, giving them a unique touch. So if a chef enjoyed cooking with meat, they could purely focus on it and as a result become a specialist in that space.[42]

But let's go back to Amna Khala for a moment. She told me that she had learned most of her cooking from her mother, who'd use nothing but clay pots and wooden planks to cook food – possibly at a time when cooking gas wasn't commonly available. The use of clay does change the flavour and fragrance of the final dish.

Today, one can find korma in most Indian restaurants. But the offering is usually just a basic mutton curry with adjusted spices and flavours. It lacks depth and texture, which comes only with cooking the meat over a low flame.

Rampuri korma is different because it uses kaskas (poppy seeds) and dry fruit in the gravy. Ghosht taar korma gets its name from its dry fruit rich gravy, luxuriously slow-cooked for hours. The other important element is the usage of animal stock instead of plain water to cook the dish. Stock water is not commonly used in home cooking because making it is a time-consuming process. However, a good stock can do wonders to a dish. It usually involves combining bones and other spices in a pot full of water, boiling it till what remains is a flavourful reduction. But since this process takes many hours, I'm guessing this won't go down well with your mother, who is likely to accuse you of finishing the house's cooking gas in one sitting! Another crucial element in making this dish is to select the meat from the legs of the animal, because they make the best korma, and a Rampuri korma would fail without succulent meat in its rich gravy. I had asked Osama Bhai whether tomatoes are used in Rampuri korma and he answered in the negative. He told me that the tanginess of the gravy is because of the curd.

Amna Khala was not done complaining about life's intricacies. This time she ranted to me about how girls today don't take an interest in cooking. I giggled and said, 'Khala, the times have changed. Now they are focusing on making money, so that they can pay chefs like us to cook for them.'

It was when I caught Abbi waving at me, his way of checking if I was ready to leave, that I realized how much time I'd spent talking to Amna Khala. For a party that I had been dreading, I had sure had an amazing time. I wanted to go on chatting with her, listening to her stories and stumbling across new recipes, but I had to leave. Amna Khala seemed to recognize the reluctance on my face and with a smile told me that if I cooked korma for her, she'd tell me more of her secret recipes. I told her it was a challenge I'd happily accept.

---

## Recipe

Serves: 4
Cooking time: 100 to 120 minutes

### Ingredients

#### *For the spice mix*

- 4–5 green cardamoms
- 2 black cardamoms
- 1-inch cinnamon
- ¼ tsp mace
- 2 star anise
- 5 cloves
- 10 black peppers
- 2–3 Kashmiri chillies
- 1 tbsp cashew nuts

#### *For the gravy*

- 3 tbsp ghee
- 2 bay leaves
- 2 tbsp ginger–garlic paste
- 1 tbsp green chilli paste
- 1 kg mutton (preferably thighs)
- ½ tsp turmeric powder
- 1 tbsp garam masala

- Salt to taste
- 6 tbsp curd, whisked
- 5 tbsp fried onion paste
- 500 ml mutton stock or water
- A pinch of saffron mixed in 1 tbsp lukewarm milk

## Method

1. In a pan, dry roast all the ingredients of the spice mix till they release their fragrance. Grind it into a fine powder using a mortar and pestle, or a mixer grinder. Keep it aside.
2. In a deep pan, heat ghee and then add the bay leaves. Add the ginger–garlic and green chilli paste, and sauté for a minute.
3. Add the mutton pieces and cook on a high flame for 10–12 minutes till they are evenly brown.
4. Add the turmeric and salt to cook on low heat for 10–12 minutes.
5. Toss in the spice mix, fried onion paste and whisked curd, and cook for 5–8 minutes or till the oil separates.
6. Add mutton stock or water, cover the vessel with a lid and cook on a low flame for 30–40 minutes, till the mutton is well-cooked and tender.
7. Open the lid and add the saffron milk and garam masala. Cook for another 10–15 minutes.
8. Serve hot with sheermal or naan.

# 19

# Khubani Malai Kofta

IT IS NOT DIFFICULT to get me into action mode if a plan involves exploring a food or coffee shop. Among my friends, I'm usually the first one to agree to go on food tours happening in town. So when my friend Shruti called on a lazy Sunday morning to check if I wanted to visit Namak Mandi in Vasant Kunj, I agreed immediately. Namak Mandi is a restaurant owned by chef extraordinaire and Padma Shri winner Imitiaz Qureshi. If you ever come across a place that has his name on it, you can be rest assured that the food will be amazing. He does not just create food, he creates a memory that stays on your palate forever.

We met at Namak Mandi for lunch. Shruti is a vegetarian, so I ordered a few vegetarian dishes to share. We ordered kofta dilkhush and mandi ki dal paired with tandoori naan. The kofta was deep-fried dumplings of seasonal vegetables cooked in a rich, creamy gravy, while the other was a slow-cooked urad dal. Both these dishes were so delicious that I took multiple servings, briefly forgetting that I was a meat eater. The kofta dilkhush came as a surprise because one almost always encounters only malai kofta on menus. The term 'kofta' comes from the classical Persian verb *kōftan* which means 'to beat' or to mince. Kofta is popular around the world and every culture seems to have its own variation. The West has meatballs, which is another variation of kofta. In a way, the famous manchurian that we get on the streets of India is another form of kofta, cooked in a spicy tomato gravy with a little Chinese touch to it. Ex-IAS officer and author Pratibha Karan writes in her book *Biryani* about the many different variations and versions of biryani. One such biryani is called 'rose biryani', which she claims to be from Lucknow. The dish is unique for its use of small meatballs, instead of the usual chunks of meat, and is topped up with rose water and dried rose petals.[43]

Although, kebabs, koftas and tikkis are made out of minced meat, there is a fine distinction between them. According to Ammi, traditionally tikkis are shallow fried, whereas koftas are deep fried and may or not be dipped in a gravy, while kebabs can be made out of whole chunks of meat. I guess all minced meat dishes have the same purpose – to use the leftover or unwanted meat and not waste any part of an animal. Koftas like nargisi kofta and malai kofta have different methods of preparation – one is just fried and served with chutney, whereas the latter is fried and then cooked in a gravy. But what left me confused is the famous galawati kebab from Lucknow. Is it a kebab or a tikki? I still don't have an answer for it.

Most of the time, vegetarian kofta dishes include paneer (cottage cheese) in it. Nuts and dry fruit are added when it's a special occasion, and once were also an indicator of the wealth of a family. As per a report, people during the Kusana and Saka Satavahana periods (75–300 CE) also used to consume a solid mass, whose description seems to be the earliest reference to the present-day paneer. One of the unique Iranian nomadic cheese was called 'Paneer-khiki'. It was originally developed by the 'Bakhtiari' tribe that resided in Iranian cities of Isfahan in the summer and Shiraz in the winter. The literal meaning of 'paneer' is container and 'khiki' is skin. The salted version of 'paneer-khiki' was known as 'paneer-e-shour'. It is indigenous to South Asia and was first introduced in India by Afghan and Iranian travellers.[44]

After catching up with Shruti and our fabulous meal, I came home completely inspired to cook malai kofta. Most north Indian households always have the ingredients for this dish in their kitchens. I began with the basics – mashing paneer for the kofta and cooking the tomato-based gravy. For the stuffing, I chopped the khubani (apricot), as well as a few other roasted dried fruit. There is a recipe for aloobokhara kofta in the book *Classic Cooking of Punjab* by Jiggs Kalra and Pushpesh Pant, which mixes lauki (bottle gourd) with aloobokhara (plum). This sounded interesting to me as I do not really enjoy lauki. Ammi has tried feeding me lauki in different forms, sweet and savory both, but I simply haven't grown to like it. She used to tell me that our Prophet loved the vegetable, to which I would say that he was welcome to eat it, but why did I have to eat something that he enjoyed? But perhaps, this recipe with plums could just change my mind about the vegetable.

Once, the dish was cooked, I found it rather similar to the ones that I have had in the past. But thinking about how pretty much every curry dish in the north has almost the same spices, I realized that it is the main ingredient as well the temperature of different gravies that changes everything in a dish, whether it is meatball spaghetti from Italy or our Indian malai kofta, or even butter chicken, which primarily has tomatoes and dairy.

## Recipe

Serves: 4

Cooking time: 70 minutes

### Ingredients

- 50 gm potato
- 100 gm paneer
- 2–3 green chillies
- 1-inch ginger
- 2 tbsp fresh coriander
- 2 tbsp apricots, chopped
- Salt to taste
- 1 tsp red chilli powder
- 2 tsp cornflour
- 1 tsp chaat masala

### *For the gravy*

- 120 gm tomato
- 2 green chillies, chopped
- 20–25 cashews, soaked
- 2 tbsp green coriander, finely chopped
- 1 tsp ginger paste
- 1 tsp cumin seeds
- ½ tsp turmeric powder
- ½ tsp red chilli powder
- ½ tsp garam masala
- 1 tsp coriander powder
- 2–3 tbsp ghee
- Salt to taste

## Method

1. In a deep pan, boil the potatoes.
2. Peel and mix the potatoes with paneer, green chilli, ginger, coriander leaves, chaat masala, red chilli powder and salt.
3. Sprinkle the cornflour into the paneer mix and knead it well.
4. Make small, bite-size balls and stuff them with small pieces of chopped apricots.
5. Deep fry the balls and keep them aside on a tissue paper.
6. Make a fine puree out of the tomatoes and green chillies.
7. Grind the soaked cashews into a smooth paste.
8. In a non-stick pan, heat the ghee and add the cumin seeds. Once they splutter, gently pour in the tomato and chilli puree. Cook for 5–8 minutes on a medium flame.
9. Add cashew paste, ginger paste, coriander powder and turmeric powder and mix well.
10. Toss in all the other spices together with salt and let them cook for 15–20 minutes. Stir well ensuring that the gravy does not get burned.
11. Once the gravy is ready, add the kofta balls, and cook for 3–4 minutes.
12. Sprinkle some leftover garam masala and adjust the seasoning if necessary.
13. Add the freshly chopped coriander and mix well.
14. Serve hot with paratha or puri.

# 20

# Kursi Miyana

ONE DAY, AS I was idly channel surfing, I stumbled upon a show on Epic Channel called *Lost Recipes*. It was hosted by model turned chef Aditya Bal and he was talking about a Hyderabadi dish I'd never heard of before. I was fascinated. I immediately rang up Bilal Bhai to check if Nisar Aunty knew anything about the dish. When he called me back to tell me she did, I almost fell off my chair. It was apt, because the dish's name also had the word 'chair' in it.

The dish, called kursi miyana, which literally translates to 'chair' or 'something to sit on', is a mince-stuffed boiled egg. I couldn't wait to find out more, so I told Bilal Bhai that I was coming right over to discuss the dish with them.

On my way to Bilal Bhai's house, I passed by a small one-room house, its main door facing the lane. The door, which was usually kept open, allowed me a glimpse into the life of its occupants. One unkept bed with one mattress on the floor, while on the walls hung a mosquito net, bedsheets, old worn-out clothes, and pictures of gods and goddess. Behind the door was a small kitchen in which every evening I found the family cooking food, the aroma of their rustic style of cooking hanging in the air. The main door was the only ventilation for the house and, whether it was their stories, memories or smoke, everything stayed in. It was chaotic poetry. The chaos reminded me that much as we ascribe meaning to things around us, everything is in fact hollow. As I walked farther towards my destination, I started thinking of Hyderabad and the kind of dishes that have come from this state. I remembered a poem written by Sarojni Naidu on Hyderabad, '... Over the city bridge Night comes majestical/Borne like a queen to a sumptuous festival.' Hyderabad is truly a majestic place and I find the languages spoken there, whether it is Telegu or the famous Hyderabadi Urdu, fascinating. Hyderabad as a city was established in 1518 by Sultan Quli Qutb-ul-Mulk, who declared independence from the Bahmani Sultanate and established the fortress city of Golconda, pronouncing himself the Sultan Quli Qutb Shah. He named the city he established as 'Bhagyanagar' after his favourite mistress 'Bhagmati', who was a dancer in the court. The sultan not only gave her a special place in his heart but also dedicated the entire city to her. Bhagmati later went on to embrace Islam and changed her name to Hyder Mahal, which resulted in the city's name changing from Bhagynagar to Hyderabad.[45]

When I got to Bilal Bhai's house, I found Nisar Aunty excitedly waiting for me. '*Bahut dino baad aaye, beta, kidhar masroof the* (Where have you been all this while)?' she said, as she gave me a glass of khus sherbet and we sat down to talk. She was very curious to know where I'd heard about kursi miyana as it was a rather rare dish. I told her about the show and asked her how she had come to know of it. She could not remember exactly but told me that she had probably learned it from her mother, and that she was willing to show me how it was done.

This beautiful dish is in fact a deep-fried egg stuffed with keema, but what makes it specifically kursi miyana is the fact that it has a skewer pierced through it, giving it the appearance of a *palki* (palanquin). According to the food writer and researcher Anwar Ali Khan, this recipe could be from the kitchens of Nawab Mahboob Ali Pasha, the sixth nizam who ruled Hyderabad between 1860–70. He gave his chefs the freedom to experiment with dishes, encouraging them to bring new things to the table. It is said that there would be competitions between the chefs during the Nizami era, with the most creative chef receiving a handsome prize. This dish was possibly created during that time.[46]

Nisar Aunty took me to her kitchen where she pulled out an old, black *kadahi* and a saucepan. She poured water into the saucepan and mixed it with vinegar and salt, giving it a nice swirl. In this, she added eight whole eggs and put it on boil. As she set out to make the keema, and I chopped the onions, Nasir Aunty told me a story. Once, Mulla Nasiruddin was invited by the king to dinner. That night, there was keema on the menu. As they ate, the king asked Mulla Nasiruddin if he liked the keema, and the Mulla replied, '*Bahut hi umda hai, huzur* (It is very good, my King).' The king, however, said he did not like it. '*Ji, bilkul, mere sarkar, kafi dheela tha* (I agree, my king, it was quite awful),' said the Mulla. The king grew angry. Why did he keep changing his mind? The Mulla had a ready reply. He said, 'I live to serve the king, not the keema.' I cracked up; Nasir Aunty's story took me right back to my childhood when my parents, my brother and I would huddle around our small black-and-white TV, watching the Mulla Nasiruddin series. It was nothing less than a laughter riot. I loved the way Nisar Aunty told me stories within stories. I had come to learn about kursi miyana, but also got reintroduced to Mulla Nasiruddin as a bonus.

Once the keema was ready, we halved the boiled eggs and stuffed the keema into them. Dipping these eggs in our prepared batter, which essentially was egg white, salt and pepper, we then deep-fried them. With the leftover keema, we made keema mattar (keema with peas), a popular dish in my house especially during the winters. The keema we made was on the drier side because it was for the purpose of stuffing. In fact, during my hostel days at Imdad Manzil, all the Muslim food joints on the street outside would sell keema mattar. Most of it would come with a thick layer of oil or fat floating on top and the dish would have the strong flavours of ginger, garlic and black pepper. Back in 2009, in Ranchi, a plate of keema mattar would cost us ₹7 to ₹10 only. It was light on the pocket but heavy on the stomach, which did the trick nicely for us students.

Keema is part of many international cuisines, but unlike in the West, Indian keema usually uses lemon, rather than chopped tomatoes or puree, to give it tartness. There are different ways of making keema. The traditional method was to hammer the meat, thereby breaking up the tissues, making the meat more tender and softer than machine-minced meat. This is still alive in some parts of Kashmir. One can also use a knife to shred the meat. Essentially, the word '*keema*' or '*qeema*' is an Urdu word for minced meat. It comes from the Persian '*qeymeh*' or the Turkish word '*kiyma*'. Traditionally, only goat meat was used to make keema because of its rich texture and natural flavour, but today one can easily find minced chicken, fish or any other red meat. There's even soya keema for vegetarians. Dishes made of minced meat were an essential part of the Mughal diet; the royal khansamas conjured up endless versions of keema that included kebabs and tikkis, to name a few.

Two hours later, we emerged from the kitchen to enjoy the fruits of our labour. I slid the eggs off the wooden skewer and dipped them into some green chutney. I took a bite of this old and almost lost dish, and it sent me spiralling. As the crispy egg skin released the soft keema inside, I wondered what the chef had been thinking when he first created this dish, and how his first diners had reacted to it. Could there be a connection between kursi miyana, nargisi kofta, scotch egg and deviled egg? They essentially all have the same ingredients – egg and minced meat. Perhaps if we dig deep into the pages of our rich food history, we'd find a link.

As I ate our kursi miyana, I felt a pang in my heart for all the recipes, both marvellous and odd, that we have lost with the passing of time. Losing them means losing their stories. I wondered if I could find a way to find and preserve them, so that they could tell their stories to others like me.

## Recipe

Serves: 2
Cooking time: 60 to 70 minutes

### Ingredients

- 4 hard-boiled eggs
- 2 tbsp ghee
- 3 tbsp onion, chopped
- 10 cloves of garlic, crushed
- 1-inch ginger, diced
- 1 tsp turmeric powder
- 100 gm minced mutton
- Water as required
- 2 green chillies
- 1½ tbsp red chilli powder

- Salt to taste
- 1 lemon
- 4 tbsp flour
- 2 egg whites
- Oil to fry

**Method**

1. Heat ghee in a *kadahi*.
2. Add the onion, ginger and garlic, and cook for 5 minutes. Add in turmeric and mix it well.
3. Toss in the washed and minced mutton. Add some water and cook for 8–10 minutes on a high flame.
4. Add the green chillies and chilli powder with salt according to taste.
5. Cook over a low flame till the mutton is well-cooked and the water has evaporated. Once the meat mixture is ready, add lemon juice and keep it aside, allowing it to cool.
6. In another bowl, make a batter of flour with ½ teaspoon of red chilli powder, salt and 1 egg white.
7. De-shell all the boiled eggs, split them lengthwise and take out the yolks.
8. Add the yolks to the minced mutton and mix well.
9. Fill this mixture into the egg cavity and seal it with the flour paste.
10. Pierce a wooden skewer into the centre of the egg (it will look like a palanquin).
11. Roll the eggs in beaten egg white and fry for a few minutes till they turn golden brown. Take them off the heat.
12. Serve hot with green chutney and onion rings.

# Brand New World

# 21

# Amrood aur Seb ki Kadhi

TRAVELLING HAS ALWAYS MEANT different things to different people, but one thing that everyone can agree upon is that travel helps us discover new places and, more importantly, oneself. For me, travelling is much more than seeing a new place. It means living life on the edge. I don't just like to travel, I like to really uncover a place and so I prefer calling myself an explorer. Exploration helps you understand culture and history through its people, places and food. My obsession with exploration has made me travel the length and breadth of our beautiful country. I have met many interesting people and learned their incredible stories through my travels. Their stories have helped me grow and respect the different customs and beliefs of people. Once, while travelling through the interiors of Madhya Pradesh, I met a hakim who was curing someone's stomach ache over the telephone. He asked his patient to keep the phone close to his ear and with his index finger touch his belly button. He recited a few verses and *duas*, and then asked the patient to slowly drink some water. Once the patient followed all the instructions, the hakim asked him how he was feeling and, to my surprise, the patient said he was feeling much better. I don't know the science behind this treatment, but what mattered most in that situation was that the person was looked after.

In May 2016, I got a chance to visit Khajuraho, the temple town famous for its Kamasutra temples, in the Bundelkhand region of Madhya Pradesh. Interestingly, the trip introduced me to a completely different and unique form of kadhi. That's when I learned that sometimes there is so much more to mundane things than the obvious.

I reached Khajuraho early in the morning and found an auto at the bus stop to take me to my accommodation. I was staying at a hostel within walking distance of the main temples. The hosts were welcoming, helping me with information regarding travel and food around the city. He also offered access to the hostel's kitchen to cook my own food. I was sharing a room with two other travellers, Noam from Israel and Justin from the United States.

Excited to explore the city, I ate a quick breakfast and headed out with a few other people from the hostel. First, we visited the temples, a sight to behold in the morning sunshine. They were built between 950–1050 CE during the reign of the Chandela dynasty, who claimed to be the direct descendants of the moon ('Chand-ela' means 'from the moon'). After their decline in the thirteenth century, the temples were left unattended and soon a dense growth of date palm closed in on them. These palms are what gave this city – called Vatsa in ancient times – its name, as 'khajur' means date.[47]

Back at the hostel, weary and full of stories from our day, we lost ourselves in discussion and didn't realize that it was almost dinner time – we had no food to eat. My roommates suggested we each cook something so that we'd have enough food for everyone. Excited, we stepped out to the closest grocery store to gather supplies.

I came back with a bag of rice, a big box of curd and half a kilo of dal vadi (lentil nuggets). The others had brought with them a haul of fruits, vegetables and bread to make salad, pudding and other dishes. Together, we had enough ingredients for dinner. I wanted to impress my new friends with something other than the usual butter chicken. I decided to stick to my comfort food, which is kadhi chawal. Inspired, I deviated from the usual kadhi with dal vadi, and tossed in some of the fruit the others had brought back. I felt that the texture of the apples and guavas would complement the tang of the kadhi. I made steamed rice, tossed with ghee, cumin and fresh coriander to accompany the kadhi. It was a hit; I saw people go back for multiple servings.

Dinner that night was a fun mix of strange and delicious dishes. None of our dishes were authentic but every dish was unique and personal to us. After eating we talked, sang songs and recited poetry late into the night.

There are certain dishes in the world that only mothers can do justice to, and kadhi chawal, a quintessential comfort food in most parts of north India, is one of them. Everyone I've met claims that their mother makes the best version of this dish, and it's possible that this is one of the reasons that restaurants don't usually include it on their menus. Who wants to compete with *maa ke haath ka khaana* (food cooked by your mother)?

There are many variations of this dish – Sindhi, Punjabi, Gujarati, Rajasthani. All of them are unique, and yet they have some features, such as the curd base and gram flour, in common. The kadhi itself could be sweet or tangy, it could have pakoras or be served plain with some fried curry leaves.

Two of my favourite variations are the Sindhi and Marwari styles of kadhi. The flavour of the base is different in both. Sindhis use kokum or tamarind to add extra sourness and throw in potatoes, drumsticks and other seasonal vegetables, while the Marwari preparation has an extra *tadka* (tempering) of ghee with spices like asafoetida, cumin and red chilli, among others. This kadhi also features either onion or dal pakoras in it.

Ammi usually makes Marwari-style kadhi with a slightly thicker consistency than the ones I have had elsewhere. She also adds a little aamchur for a dash of tang. Abbi likes his plate with extra papad and a little dollop of ghee on top of the rice.

Kadhi originated in the dry lands of Rajasthan. Bisma Tirmizi records that the scarcity of ingredients, including vegetables and water, in the region had a profound effect on the diet – locals relied heavily on milk and milk-based products. The region is dry but nevertheless rich culturally, and this is reflected in their food as well. The food was also influenced by the desert gypsies and travellers who could carry only a limited weight and hence, prepared dishes that could last long without going bad. Bisma Tirmizi writes in *Dawn*, '[In the] deserts of Rajasthan, the use of lentils, gram flour and beans obtained from native plants were used extensively for cooking, so the evolution of karhi had to happen. The neighbouring states of Punjab, Gujarat and Haryana borrowed the besan karhi pakora from Rajasthan and gave it a flavour of their own.'[48]

I came back to Delhi with new friendships and new stories to narrate, but soon forgot about the dish. One weekend, a few months later, Ammi was making kadhi. I stopped her and took over the kitchen. Ammi had no clue what I was up to, but I had a feeling she didn't particularly want to cook that day as she surrendered the kitchen to me rather easily. I replicated the dish, adding a few spoons of roasted almond paste.

Ammi was impressed with my offering. She told me it was a flavour and texture bomb exploding in her mouth. A little sweet, a little tangy and just a sliver of spice, with a texture that was simultaneously rough and smooth. All in one spoonful. She asked me what this dish was called, and I decided to christen it 'Shahi Amrood Seb ki Kadhi'. And since it had my mother's approval, it soon became one of my signature dishes and a hit in our family.

This dish was later added to the menu of one of the restaurants where I used to work. I can now add different flavours and textures of my own preference to make a new dish because travel helps me learn new techniques and teaches me to think on my feet.

## Recipe

Serves: 2
Cooking time: 40 to 45 minutes

### Ingredients

- ¾ tbsp gram flour (besan)
- ½ cup thick sour curd
- 2 pinches salt
- ½ cup water
- A pinch of powdered turmeric
- 3 tbsp cashew paste
- 1½ tbsp ghee
- A pinch of asafoetida
- 1 bay leaf
- ¼ tsp mustard seeds
- 2 red chillies, chopped
- 1 tsp red chilli powder
- 1 apple, peeled and sliced

- 1 big guava, de-seeded and sliced
- 2 masala dal vadi

## Method

1. In a blender, add the besan, curd, turmeric, salt and water. It should be of pouring consistency because if it is too thick, it will destroy the base.
2. Strain and transfer to a pan. Stir constantly over medium heat while bringing it to a boil.
3. Add the cashew paste and cook till the rawness disappears. This is the kadhi base.
4. In a small pan, heat ½ tablespoon of ghee and add the asafoetida, bay leaf, mustard seeds and red chillies.
5. Add this tadka to the kadhi and let it cook for 3–4 minutes.
6. Meanwhile, add ghee in a pan and then the sliced apples. Toss in chilli powder and salt to taste. Sauté for 2–3 minutes.
7. In another pan, deep fry the masala vadi till they become brown, crispy and easy to crush.
8. Add the apples, vadi and raw guava into the curd mixture. Let it simmer for 2 minutes.
9. Remove the pan from heat and serve with either steamed rice or with khubba roti.

## 22

# Paneer aur Kachi Kairi ka Tikka

THERE ARE A FEW journeys that have really stood out during my travels. What made these journeys memorable for me were the people I met and the stories they told me.

Once, I was travelling to Ahmedabad in the dead of summer for work. It was hot enough to cook an egg on the simmering streets. After I was done with work, I headed straight to the market and *mandis* of Ahmedabad. The first ever food coma that I have ever had was in this city. I was advised to try the food at Sasuji's or the House of MG. Both these places are famous for their unlimited traditional vegetarian thalis – a complete meal with many dishes served in small quantities accompanied by snacks, roti and khichdi. I love thalis because there is something for everyone and a perfect balance of flavour. Salty, sweet, tangy, dry, crunchy, with gravy – a thali's got it all.

The next day, bored with work, I rang a friend, Roomani, who lived in the city and we decided to make a day of it. Roomani took me to all the tourist hotspots such as Law Garden, which is full of food, local clothes and wall hangings; Manek Chowk is a unique place because in the morning it is a wholesale market of jewellery, spices, clothes and few other essentials, but in the evening, it transforms into a lane full of food stalls busy till 4 a.m.; a few temples; Swati Snacks, another common hangout for the locals; and other places she loved. We took a break at a shop that sold mango milkshakes to try their aam ras (a sweet beverage made by grinding ripe mangoes with milk), which turned out to be the thickest and freshest I have ever had. I pecked through the day, eating everything from an eggless omelette (a dish made of chickpea flour that looks like an omelette) to fusion Mexican Gujarati food. At around 7 p.m., still hungry, I asked Roomani if we could try something different, perhaps something from a home kitchen. After some thought, Roomani told me she knew just the place and made a phone call.

She took me to her friend's house, whose mother she said makes amazing, mouth-watering food. She called him to let him know she was coming over with a crazy foodie from Delhi.

We drove to old Ahmedabad through the busy traffic. This part of town had narrow lanes with cars and bikes parked on the streets, making it difficult to move around, but it had a feel similar to that of Old Delhi. After driving and dodging the roadblocks for almost an hour we finally arrived at her friend Aadil's house. The flat was on the fourth floor and the lift wasn't working. I told myself this was a great way to build my appetite.

Aadil and his family welcomed us warmly. They were jewellery merchants by profession and lived in a tastefully appointed apartment. We sat down with cups of masala chai as we talked. With my love for food, I think I find it easy to initiate a conversation with the main chefs of the house, usually mothers. Aadil's mother was no different. We exchanged stories about our love for food. Traditionally, a Gujarati thali includes a combination of fried, stir-fried, blanched and boiled dishes, as well as a curry in a rich, silky, sweet sauce. It will also come with a sweet dal, shaak/sabzi, roti, rice and khichdi. Every item on the thali is subtly flavoured to maintain an overall balance, ensuring that none of the spices overpower each other. I've always wondered why Gujarati dishes are usually sweet, and, as it turns out, it's to do with the region's climate. Aadil told me that since temperatures often go up to 50 degrees Celsius, and the weather is quite dry, it is important to stay hydrated. Ingredients like sugar and salt, lemon and tomatoes, which are used in many dishes here, help the body retain electrolytes in the extreme weather.

Upon my insistence, Aadil's mother took me to her kitchen to show me her cache of spices. Her kitchen was large and airy, and everything was perfectly arranged. It was almost like a professional kitchen. Her range of spices was unparalleled; her kitchen almost like a supermarket. There were different sections for lentils and staples, spices, tea and coffee, utensils, cutlery and crockery. She told me about an interesting custom of a few Gujarati families, including hers, which is to consume moong dal on Wednesdays. Food historian K.T. Achaya writes in his book, *Indian Food: A Historical Companion*, that pulses such as maash (urad), mansura (masoor) and mudga (moong) are mentioned in the Yajur Veda. Ayurveda suggests that the moong bean is a power-packed lentil because it corrects the three major doshas – *vata, pitta* and *kapha* – of the human body. As per Indian astrology, Wednesday is ruled by the planet Mercury and moong dal is eaten on this day to please the planet.[49]

Usually they ate non-vegetarian food and were fond of biryani, but she was making an exception as it was easy for me to find kebabs and biryani in Delhi. Gujarat is famous for its vegetarian dishes and I was keen to see what she came up with. That day, she was making paneer aur kachi kairi ka tikka. She had made her own paneer because she didn't trust the quality of store-bought ingredients. She mixed all the spices in a big copper plate and added the paneer to it, leaving it to marinate for half an hour, so that it absorbed all the flavours. She added a cashew and pine nut paste to the spice mix batter to give her dish a royal touch, and fried onion paste because her family loved its flavour. What was surprising was the addition of a char-roasted raw mango puree; it gave the dish a wonderful tangy yet smoky flavour. She told me that the perfect tikka requires patience, and that cooking should be a fun and therapeutic activity. '*Jaldi ka kaam shaitan ka* (Haste makes waste).'

The reluctant founder of the Mughal dynasty was also responsible for the birth of the tikka. Babur loved eating meat, but was afraid of choking on chicken bones. He ordered his khansama to de-bone the chicken before it went into the tandoor and also serve him bite-sized pieces. This resulted in '*joleh*' (Persian for tikka). The recipe was further improvised by adding a yoghurt marinade as well as other spices. If you travel around Delhi today, you will find thousands of food vendors serving lip-smacking tikkas. All north Indian restaurants will almost always have them on their menu.

Very soon, the smell of tikkas being made was enough to make the entire family hungry and impatient. Aadil and his sister set the table, while his mother and I started bringing the dishes out to the table. The tikka was one of its kind. The aroma of masalas and the flavour of raw mango made my taste buds dance. We ate to our heart's content.

Tikkas tend to be non-vegetarian traditionally, but this paneer aur kachi kairi ka tikka was a unique vegetarian take on this popular dish.

As much as I enjoyed the tikka, a part of me was focused on the leftover dry masala. I was not sure if it was proper to ask to get the powder packed, but I gathered my courage and as I was walking out of the house I asked, '*Aunty, woh joh masala bach gaya tha, kya aap mujhe thoda sa doge* (Would you please give me that leftover spice mix)?' I had already turned red, afraid she'd judge me, but thankfully I have had it easy with the main chefs of any family as they tend to like me for my love for food. Aunty laughed at my question first and said, '*Arrey, le kar jao tum, aur bana du kya* (Yes of course, should I make some more for you)?'

Till date I hold that spice mix as my benchmark while attempting to replicate the dish.

I think this is why one must travel. It is not just the actual travel or the photos you capture, the landscape you cover or the people you meet, but it is a mix of all these factors that makes travelling a beautiful journey. All you see becomes a part of you and stays with you forever. I am reminded of a quote by Jawaharlal Nehru, which I believe captures the essence of travelling: 'We live in a wonderful world that is full of beauty, charm and adventure. There is no end to the adventures we can have if only we seek them with our eyes open.'

## Recipe

Serves: 2
Cooking time: 55 to 60 minutes

### Ingredients

- 500 gm paneer (cottage cheese), cubes
- 1 tsp red chilli powder
- 2 tbsp ginger–garlic paste
- 1 tsp coriander powder
- ½ tsp garam masala powder

- 1 tsp cumin seeds, crushed
- Yellow food colour as required
- 3 tbsp kachi kairi (raw mango) pulp
- 1 tbsp lemon juice
- Salt to taste
- Koyla (charcoal) for smoke
- 2 tbsp ghee

## Method

1. In a bowl, mix in the red chilli powder, coriander powder, garam masala, cumin seeds, food colour, mango pulp, lemon juice, ginger–garlic paste and adjust the salt. Mix it well into a paste.
2. Prick the paneer pieces and marinate them in the paste for 30 minutes.
3. Take the hot charcoal in a bowl, add ghee and place it in the marinade bowl. Let it smoke for 5–7 minutes.
4. Oil a grill or normal non-stick pan and grill the paneer on a low flame until done.
5. Serve hot with chutney or eat it by itself.

# 23

# Bhopali Mutton Rezala

MY FRIEND ALTAF LIVES in Ibrahimpura in the old city of Bhopal. The street he lives on is always heavy with the aroma of food, either bread or kebabs, and one of the most famous places for kebabs here is Jameel Hotel. Altaf lived in a traditional old house that opened into a courtyard with a verandah running along its sides. Shafi Uncle, Atlaf's father, was sitting on a wooden *charpai* on the verandah.

'*Ama Khan, aaj-kal kya chal riya hai* (What's going on)?' he called out to me. Shafi Uncle reminded me of Surma Bhopali from my favourite movie *Sholay*. This is how elders in Bhopal will speak to you. He was rolling a paan from an old aluminium box, which reminded me of my Nani and Dadi. For Bhopalis, paan-making is an art and Shafi Uncle had mastered it. He told me, '*Hamare hatho ka Bhopali paan khao, miya, duniya ke tamam paan ko bhool jaoge* (Try my paan and you'll forget all the other paans of the world).' I am no connoisseur of this leafy mouth freshener, but I was really impressed with the way he was making paan. It was art to my eyes.

I sat with Shafi Uncle while Altaf ran a few errands. I came to realize that Shafi Uncle loved talking about his city. Did I know that Bhopal was ruled by women? Did I know that it was originally called Bhojpal after the Parmara King Bhoj and the dam (*pala*) that was built to secure his eastern frontiers in the eleventh century? In fact, one can still find the 32-feet-tall statue of Raja Bhoj in the middle of Bada Talab (upper lake).

According to author Shaharyar M. Khan, the city as we know it today was transformed by one of Emperor Aurangzeb's Afghan soldiers, Dost Mohammed Khan, who was handling the Malwa area of Madhya Pradesh before but took charge of this part after Aurangzeb's death in 1707. After Khan's death in 1740, Bhopal was ruled by one of the most celebrated begums of Bhopal, Qudsia Begum, who took charge of the city on 13 November 1819 as a regent after her husband, Nazar Mohammed Khan, who ruled Bhopal for just three years and five months, was assassinated. A rebel and a strong leader, Qudsia Begum was among the few women in Indian history who refused to follow the purdah system. She also became the first woman to govern the city, followed by her daughter Sikander Begum in 1847. This female rulership lasted uninterrupted for almost 107 years.[50]

Later, Altaf took me around town for a spin, showing me the sights and sounds. Bhopal's street food, like achar gosht, keema pulao, rogan josh, to name a few, can leave you spoiled for choice. Altaf had warned me not to eat too much as his father was making Bhopali mutton rezala for dinner. There was no way I was going to miss out on his old man's experience and expertise. When we returned, our appetites raging, Shafi Uncle was waiting for us.

Shafi Uncle took me to his kitchen where he gave me some onions and chillies to chop, saying, '*Ama Khan, khane ke liye thodi to mehnat karni padti hai* (You'll have to put in some labour to enjoy the food).' Meanwhile, he started preparing the dish by chopping up the mutton. He had learned this recipe from his wife, who had passed away 20 years ago, when Altaf was just seven. '*Mujhe usse kuch zyaada hi pyaar tha, toh dusri shaadi karke use dokha nahi dena chahta tha* (I loved her too much to betray her memory by getting married again),' he told me, his eyes shimmering with love and nostalgia. Since then, he has been both Abbu and Amma to Altaf. He used an old copper *kadahi* to cook the dish – the one his wife would cook in when she was alive. First, he caramelized the onions in hot ghee, added a ginger–garlic paste, followed by the mutton. He told me it was important to *bhuno* (roast) the mutton over a slow flame so that the meat loses its raw smell and cooks thoroughly. While we were preparing the dish, Altaf make a quick dash to the market to get us some roomali rotis and sheermal.

Rezala is just as famous in Bengal as it is in Bhopal, the addition of posto dana (poppy seeds) distinguishing the Bengali variety. However, according to an interview with corporate chef Sarfaraz Hussain of the Shiraz Kolkata, rezala is a Mughlai dish, originally from Lucknow.[51] In Kolkata, the dish has a creamy rich, white gravy whereas in Bhopal the same dish has a striking green gravy because of the use of coriander paste. According to Marryam H. Reshii, the use of coriander in Bhopal was to mitigate indigestion that would often result from the city's hard water.[52] Coriander also gives this rezala a beautiful green colour, which is not common in this dish in general.

Music played in the background as we sat down to eat – unusual in a Muslim household. I have never seen music being played in a traditional Muslim house while eating, but Shafi Uncle was different. He loved the ghazals of Bade Ghulam Ali Khan and Nida Fazli's poetry.

The roomali rotis perfectly complemented the rich dish. It was almost 11 p.m. by the time we were done, much later than my routine dinner time. But Altaf told me that young Bhopalis don't sleep till late at night, hanging out in the streets after dinner or heading out to Chatori Gali (food street) for a late-night kebab fix. Shafi Uncle went back to his *charpai* and started making his paan.

After dinner, like a true Bhopali, Altaf took me out on his scooter to show me the city by night. It's like you are in a different city, he said. We ended up at a mosque near the Bada Talab. A hard-won peace settled around us, and suddenly I was overwhelmed by the city's beauty. I realized that in the evening people adopt an even slower pace of going about their way. They don't have work to hurry to and so will sit around with a cup of tea or at a kebab shop, and talk about everything from food to politics. I loved the vibe of the city simply because of the relaxed attitude of its people, similar to that of Old Delhi. My friend Abu Sufiyan says, '*Purani* Dilli *aisi jagah hai jahan koi kaam waqt par nahi hota, aur aisa koi kaam nahi hai jo waqt rehte nahi hota* (Old Delhi is a place where no work is done at the right time, and there is no such work which is not done).' This saying is perfect for Bhopal as well. What is the hurry to finish the work anyway? Older parts of any town seem to defy the rat race the big cities run.

## Recipe

Serves: 3 to 4
Cooking time: 110 to 130 minutes

### Ingredients

- ¼ cup ghee
- 2 large onions, finely sliced
- 2 tbsp ginger–garlic paste

- 500 gm mutton
- 1 tbsp fennel seeds
- 1 tbsp coriander seeds
- 125 gm yoghurt
- 1 tbsp cumin seeds, crushed
- 1 tbsp red chilli powder
- 1 tsp turmeric powder
- 1 tsp garam masala
- ½ tsp nutmeg and mace powder
- ½ tsp cardamom powder
- Salt to taste
- 1 cup water
- 3–4 green chillies, chopped
- 2 tbsp fresh coriander, chopped

## Method

1. In a deep pan, heat the ghee and fry the onion slices.
2. Once the onions are fried, add the ginger–garlic paste. Cook for 3–5 minutes or till the raw smell of ginger–garlic goes away.
3. Add mutton and cook over a high flame till the mutton is evenly cooked and browned.
4. Meanwhile, in a separate pan roast the coriander and fennel seeds. Once its fragrance is released and it turns light brown, take the pan off the heat and allow it to cool. Then, crush the mixture and make it into a fine powder.
5. Mix this with the mutton pieces and ensure that it is well-coated.
6. Whisk the yoghurt. Add cumin, chilli powder, turmeric, garam masala, nutmeg and mace and cardamom powder into the yoghurt.

7. Adjust the salt, mix all of it properly and cook over a high flame for 6–8 minutes.
8. Add water, cover and let it simmer over a low flame for 20–25 minutes.
9. Add the chopped chillies and fresh coriander, and cook for another 2 minutes on a high flame.
10. Serve with naan or sheermal.

# 24

# Bun Kebab

IF YOU LIVE IN the countryside, every morning you'll wake up to the chirping of birds. Equally certain is that if you're travelling by train in India, the chirping birds will be replaced by vendors selling chai and coffee, chanting '*Chai, garam chai le lo* (Tea, get some hot tea).' To some this might be noise, to others it is music to their ears.

It wasn't long before I was back in Bhopal. My friend Sneha rang me up one day and asked if I wanted to go with her to Bhopal to celebrate her flatmate's birthday. I was hesitant because I had some pending work and a trip lined up for later that week. Sensing my weakness, her flatmate, Suhani, took charge and said, 'Sadaf, you should totally come. We're going to a farmhouse – fresh vegetables to cook within a beautiful village setting. What more do you want?' She had me at fresh food and village setting. Cooking in the open has its own charm. Couple that with fresh produce, and there's magic. The idea excited me so I agreed. It was only when she booked my ticket that I realized I was one among a party of five who would be travelling together. My tickets booked, we were scheduled to travel in 10 days.

On the day of our journey, we gathered at Nizamuddin railway station and I met the others – Raunaq, the foodie, Pranava, the discount and deals guy, Anay, the serious and slightly quiet guy, and Suhani's brother, Bharat, the singer. We settled into our respective seats with boxes of pizza, soft drinks and water. This was a first for me because until then train journeys usually involved aloo bhujiya, puri and achaar, all packed into a big box with disposable plates, with samosa and pakora breaks at every other station. Once we'd finished our food, someone pulled out Monopoly and it kept us occupied till late in the evening. We were woken up early by the morning azan of the chaiwala, which made me believe that there are few things quite as satisfying as drinking tea on trains, talking to random people, the smell of home-cooked food and mango pickle, or standing beside the door of the train to feel the breeze. Soon, we were at Bhopal and took a taxi to the farmhouse.

The farmhouse was grand and sprawling, complete with a swimming pool and fields rich with home-grown vegetables. It was exactly as I had pictured it, and I was happy that my expectations had been met by reality. We were greeted by Suhani's friend, Palak's mother and an awkward, life-sized cut-out of her father. There was chai and fresh aloo parathas, which tasted much better here in the fresh air of a small town. In the evening, we were joined by another friend, Aditya, an entrepreneur and chess wizard.

The next three days were spent eating, partying and playing games. On the last day, Raunaq and I wanted to experience Bhopali food at Chatori Gali of Ibrahimpura in old Bhopal. Chatori Gali (*chatori* means glutton) is the Bhopali version of Old Delhi's Chandini Chowk. It is cramped, atmospheric, and bustling and bursting with food joints. Whole fried chicken hung on shop fronts and the scent of kebabs grew stronger as we made our way to its heart. I envied the locals who had their favourite shops and restaurants, and knew their way around its secrets.

Eventually, Raunaq and I settled for a stand run by Mohammad Faiz, a kebab vendor in his fifties.

Whether slicing the buns into halves or pouring chutney over the kebabs, Faiz was exceptionally quick and precise in his movements. It wasn't long before we had struck up a conversation. 'Khan, *ye Chatori Gali toh abhi famous hui, lekin asli naam to iska Gali Madina Hotel Wali hai* (This street might be famous as Chatori Gali, but we all know it as Gali Madina Hotel Wali),' he said. Perhaps it is famous as Chatori Gali because of the sheer number of food joints. In the nineties, there was a popular restaurant called Hotel Madina, which served the best bun kebab in town. When it shut down, many small food joints rushed in to fill the vacuum, inadvertently creating this food paradise called Chatori Galli.

Mohammad Faiz had been serving kebabs at the same spot for the past 10 years. In the mornings, he drove a rickshaw, but in the evenings it was all about bun kebabs. He told us how people were relaxed come evening, which I had already learned on my last visit. An interesting tale he mentioned was how the nawabs would grill their kebabs on their swords. Later, I found out that Faiz was quite right. In the book, *On the Kebab Trail: A Moti Mahal Cookbook* by Monish Gujral, I learned that kebabs were created to meet the shortage of food supply in the Near East. Kebabs originated and had been popularized in Turkey, where soldiers would grill or smoke chunks of freshly hunted animals skewered on their swords over an open fire.[53] Faiz Bhai told us that one could find more than 40 different varieties of kebabs in Bhopal, each with its own unique flavour.

The bun kebab is a unique Bhopali sandwich, available only in the evenings and costing just ₹10 or ₹15. It is essentially hand-pounded, flattened meat kebabs, shallow-fried and placed in a bun with a generous dollop of spicy green chutney. This is once again pressed on to a flat tawa and served hot. The sweetness of the bun is a perfect complement to the spicy meat, like the pairing of sheermal with galawati.

In a bun kebab, besan is added to the meat and then hand pounded, giving it a unique texture. Faiz Bhai recognized that the new food vendors used machines to mince the meat, which does not lend it a real flavour. I agreed; before stopping at his stall, Raunaq and I had grabbed quick bites at three other places, but none could compare with Faiz Bhai's offering. The kebab on its own was delicious and reminded me of Ammi's shammi kebabs. Faiz Bhai said, '*Ye bun kebab toh* Pakistan *mein bhi famous hai* (Bun kebab is famous in Pakistan as well)' – a fact that was corroborated by my friend from Karachi, Maheenjam, a student of gender studies at the University of London, who said it was her favourite evening snack. It's a cheap snack and there are many varieties of it, the most famous being a version with a fried egg and kebab together – this was a variation I did not notice in Bhopal. She started salivating while talking to me about the dish and added that the vendors are often invited to cater for marriages or birthday parties. Maheenjam told me that in Pakistan they don't use a sweet bun, like the ones I ate in Bhopal.

Raunaq and I were lost, taking photos, eating and hopping from one food joint to another, until Sneha called to remind us that we had a train to catch. We packed an order of kebabs and rushed out of the market. Today, even though I have the recipe of the kebab and the chutney, I still think there's no matching the flavour of street food. But if you want a slice of Bhopali street fare, you can give this recipe a shot.

## Recipe

Serves: 8 to 10
Cooking time: 80 to 90 minutes

### Ingredients

- 500 gm mutton, boneless
- 200 gm channa dal/split Bengal gram, soaked for 4–6 hours
- 8–10 dried red chillies
- 1 tbsp coriander seeds
- 1 tbsp cumin seeds
- 1 egg
- 1 tsp garam masala powder
- 1½ tbsp ginger–garlic paste
- ¼ cup fresh coriander leaves
- Salt to taste
- Ghee/oil for frying
- 8–10 sweet buns
- Green chutney
- Lemon juice
- Sliced tomato, onion and green chillies to serve

### Method

1. In a pressure cooker, boil the mutton, channa dal, dried red chillies, coriander and cumin seeds for 3–4 whistles.
2. Let it cool and open the lid.
3. Then, in a blender, make a smooth paste of the contents of the pressure cooker without adding any water. The mixture must be dry.

4. In a bowl, take the mixture and crack in an egg, add garam masala, ginger–garlic paste and freshly chopped coriander leaves. Adjust the salt and seasoning.
5. Make small patties and keep it aside for 30 minutes.
6. In a shallow frying pan, heat ghee or oil and pan-fry the patties for 3–4 minutes on each side.
7. Once the patties are ready, place them between the sweet buns. Add green chutney, onion, tomato, chillies, a squirt of lemon juice and grill the buns on a pan before serving them hot.

# 25

# Achari Gosht

A FEW YEARS AGO, I travelled with some friends to Agra to see the Taj Mahal. They had never seen the marvel and I acted as their guide. They were blown away by its beauty, architecture and the science of this monumental structure. Boggling as it was to think of the effort of thousands of labourers and the investment of lakhs of rupees that went into this structure, it was the reason behind why it was built that lingered with them the most. Apart from the major monuments like Khusro Bagh, Lal Qila, Mausamman Burj and Fatehpur Sikri, Agra is also famous its *mandi*s and bazaars, and my two favourite places are the Rawatpara Spice Market and Sadar Bazaar for leather and chaat. Rawatpara is similar to Delhi's spice market, Khari Baoli, but Sadar Bazaar is a little different – it is more organized and there is ample space to walk.

I am fascinated by spices and I can never have enough of them. Be it in Delhi, Agra, Chennai or Kerala – wherever I go, I pick up the freshest spices possible. (It is a different matter that Ammi redistributes my loot to all our family members.) We walked through the Rawatpara Spice Market, watching people bargain and travellers take photographs, capturing their beautiful colours, and others going about their business. The heat was oppressive as we passed by the many petha and daalmot shops reminding us of Delhi's Aggarwal Sweets and Bikanerwala. We looked for a place to eat. Often, when I am in a new city, I feel like a hunter-gatherer. I have no idea where to find good food. A new-age hunter-gatherer would settle for a familiar McDonald's, but that hunter-gatherer would not be an explorer. On the other hand, I am an explorer and always want to eat something unique to the city I'm in. I feel it is boring to eat from a fast-food franchise, and also a little insulting to the local cuisine and ingredients. A few locals pointed us to shabby-looking places, others sent us to places that didn't exist or were shut. In hindsight, it was this confusion that made the trip exciting because it left me with stories to share. But back then, we were approaching starvation. Finally, we decided to stop at the nearest restaurant to grab a small bite before continuing our search.

The restaurant we had walked into had the usual set-up of a few wooden chairs and tables with bright red-and-white checked tablecloths, a big picture of the Taj Mahal and a few frames on the wall to brighten up the atmosphere. It looked hygienic and was well-lit. We found a table by the window and settled in. The menu consisted of Mughlai, Awadhi and Chinese options. Immediately my eyes stopped at the achari khumb (pickled mushroom) in the vegetarian section and achari mutton in the non-vegetarian section. I've always loved pickles, so I decided to try the vegetarian version.

Pickling is done to preserve an ingredient. The ingredient can be pickled in brine water, like in the West, or in spices and oil like in South Asia. As per Digital Dictionaries of South Asia, the word 'achar' finds its origin in Persian and means powdered or salted meats or fruit preserved in salt, vinegar, honey or syrup; particularly onions preserved in vinegar.[54] We Indians have taken the simple achar to a different level by pickling almost everything from mango to fish to cauliflower, and in fact, different communities have their own versions of achar mix masala. Usha R. Prabhakaran, a Chennai-based lawyer, has put together the recipes of over 1,000 pickles in her book *Usha's Pickle Digest.*[55] Pickle is a great way to add tang and flavour to insipid food. Prabhakaran also writes that pickling agents find mention in the Vedic era as well as in the medical treatises of Susruta and Charaka.[56] I am a fan of pickles. Most recently, I learned how to pickle fresh turmeric. This not only goes well with dishes but also has many health benefits and helps with heart disease, Alzheimer's and may also improve symptoms of depression and arthritis. I like to collect pickles from different states and places that I travel to, and at home, I have a whole shelf devoted to a variety of local pickles.

Achari khumb is the vegetarian version of achari gosht. Some say it is from Uttar Pradesh, while others say it is from Hyderabad or Bhopal. I asked Atul Sikand and he told me that there is a possibility that this dish originated in the Mughal kitchens and travelled to these places. Achari gosht originates from the same idea of pickling an ingredient so that it lasts longer and can be enjoyed at a later time without the flavours getting ruined. He believes that this dish was more a preserve, like an achar.

Still curious to pinpoint the origins of achari gosht, I reached out to two experts – Marryam Reshii and Vir Sanghvi – on Twitter. They both surmised that the dish was created in Hyderabad; the tangy and sour flavour was characteristic of food from the region. Ruchi Srivastava, owner of the food production company Greed Goddess Media, also agrees. She told me that Hyderabadi cuisine is partial to *khatta* (tangy) flavours and that is why the use of tamarind is more prevalent than yoghurt. Awadhi culture, on the other hand, doesn't have much *khatta* in their food, the stress being on subtle flavours such as whole spices.

In her article on achari gosht in *Dawn,* Bisma Tarmizi quotes food historian Collingham, confirming its Hyderabadi origins: 'The Bahmanid kingdom eventually broke up into a number of satellite states, one of which was Golconda, which later became known as Hyderabad. Here, the pulaos of the Persians combined with Hindu Deccani cookery, in which shredded coconut and coconut milk are vital ingredients and the tang of curry leaves, the astringent bite of fresh fenugreek leaves, and the sharp sour note of tamarind impart flavour. The meeting of the two styles gave rise to an elegant cuisine with unusual combinations, such as lamb cooked with tamarind.'[57, 58]

In Islam, there is a debate over whether mushroom is halal or haram, and because of this confusion, many Muslims, including Nanna, are unaware of the delicious taste of this simple ingredient. I checked with my friend Maulana Asrar and he debunked the idea that mushroom is haram. 'Whatever comes from the ground is allowed. They are a gift from Allah, the Almighty. He has blessed them, but one should be careful to check whether they [mushrooms] are poisonous or not.' I like the way he clarified the confusion – I'll be sure not to eat any poisonous mushrooms.

After reading so much about the dish, I wanted to cook the same dish in my kitchen, not the mushroom variety, but with mutton. I went straight to the butcher's shop to get meat with bones, which I believe is important for this dish. The pieces can be from any part of the body, but a little fat will help ensure the moisture and tenderness of the dish.

I like grinding fresh spices and I think everyone who loves cooking in general also loves to grind their own spices. I pulled out a small pan from the shelf to roast all the achari masala that I then popped into the mortar pestle. I purposefully did not grind it to a fine powder and kept it a little rough. When I began cooking, I threw in a few whole spices again; it looked beautiful and the aroma it released added to the entire dish. A lot of mutton dishes ask for the mutton to be boiled or marinated first, but this recipe asks for a good roasting before adding all the spices and water to cook. It took a little while to prepare this dish, but it was not difficult.

Ammi had placed the leftover gobi aloo from lunch and fresh paratha on the table, and I added my bowl of achari gosht. When we started eating, Abbi commented on the meat being cooked very nicely and having a distinct tang. Shabi had loaded his plate, and then said if he ate one more piece he might just burst open. With a lot of laughter in the air, the elegant achari gosht dish had done the deed of drawing together people once again.

---

## Recipe

Serves: 6
Cooking time: 120 minutes

### Ingredients

- 1 kg mutton
- 1 tbsp ginger–garlic paste
- 2 tbsp yoghurt
- 1 tsp turmeric powder
- 1 tsp coriander powder
- 1 tsp red chilli powder
- 1 tsp vinegar
- Salt to taste

***For the spice mix (A)***

- 4 dried red chillies
- 1 tsp mustard seeds

- 1 tsp cumin seeds
- 1 tsp methi seed (fenugreek seeds)
- 1 ½ tsp fennel seeds
- 1 tsp kalonji (onion seeds)

***For the gravy***

- 3 tbsp mustard oil
- 3 medium onions, sliced thin
- 3 tbsp tamarind pulp or 4 tomatoes pureed
- Water
- Fresh coriander leaves to garnish
- 1-inch ginger, julienned
- 2 green chillies

## Method

1. Wash and clean the mutton pieces, and pat them dry.
2. Marinate the mutton in ginger–garlic paste, yoghurt, turmeric, coriander and red chilli powder with vinegar and salt. Let it sit in the fridge for 6–8 hours. Overnight is ideal.
3. Take a non-stick pan and dry roast all the whole spices (A) and grind them into a coarse powder. Use a mortar and pestle if possible.
4. In another pan, heat the mustard oil till it smokes, then add the sliced onions, sautéing them for 5–7 minutes till they become translucent.
5. Add the spice mix and cook for another 2–3 minutes on a low flame. Ensure you do not burn the spices.
6. Toss in the marinated mutton pieces and sauté on a high flame for 7–10 minutes, till the mutton gets nicely coated in the spices and turns brown.

7. Add the tamarind pulp or tomato puree with the desired amount of water, depending on how you like your gravy.
8. Cover the vessel and cook the mutton on medium heat.
9. Keep stirring at regular intervals so that the meat doesn't burn, till it becomes soft and easy to bite.
10. Once the meat is cooked, sprinkle some freshly chopped coriander leaves, sliced ginger and chillies.
11. Let it rest for 30–45 minutes, then heat it once again and serve with khameeri roti.

# 26

# Chand Bibi ke Keema Kachori

ONE COLD MARCH MORNING I received a text from my friend Kalyani Khona, founder of Inclov, asking if I wanted a free stay at a fancy hotel in Lucknow for a couple of days. Before I could fully process the text she called to wake me up, screaming down the phone to get my answer. I had no choice but to agree at the time, not because I necessarily wanted to go, but because she was talking loudly and I desperately wanted to get some more sleep.

A few hours later, finally awake and fortified with coffee, I gave her a call to get a better idea of this out-of-the-blue plan. A friend of hers was getting married in Lucknow and had rooms reserved at a hotel. I needed a break from work, and she wanted company, so when the invitation was extended, I agreed. She reassured me by telling me that we had enough time to book our tickets and get our shaadi dresses sorted. For me, though, the focus was of course not the wedding but the food and narrow lanes of Aminabad and Hazratganj.

Lucknow is the birthplace of the elegant and refined Awadhi cuisine. Author and consultant chef Izzat Hussain writes that the birth of Mughlai food in the Awadhi region originated in the eighteenth century with the Nawab of Awadh. The khansamas used to cook dishes after consulting the hakims and hence, only the epicurean and sensualist nawabs and warriors of Awadh would get to taste these dishes. This has given us some enduring dishes such as galawati kebab, kakori kebab, mutanjan, kaddu ki sabzi–puri, apart from many sophisticated culinary techniques. Awadhi cuisine invented the technique of 'dum pukht' (the process of slow-cooking).[59] Writers J. Inder Singh Kalra and Pradeep Das Gupta state in their book that the innovative technique of dum pukht was born during the reign of Nawab Asaf-ud-Daula, the fourth nawab of Awadh. The technique originated in Persia, where the cooked dish would be sealed within another dish and buried in warm sand to mature its flavour. In 1784, Lucknow was struck by famine and the nawab decided to build a shrine, the Bada Imambara, to help provide employment. In order to ensure that work would be distributed among the people, the nawab had the working class build up the structure by day and destroyed by night by the elite class. During this process, the khansamas would cook food in huge quantities and keep them in big vessels, sealed and placed in double-walled *bukharis* (ovens) to ensure that the food stayed warm throughout the day.[60] As a result, India got its own version of the dum-pukht technique. Similarly, this is also where the idea of the masala potli (bag of spices) – a method where the potli is placed in a rice preparation to give it flavour and aroma without leaving whole spices in the pot – originated. 'There are no chunky pieces or whole spices floating in the gravy... this is food of the kings, kebabs have to melt in the mouth, the meats have to be tender, the gravy silky – the nawabs, after all, couldn't be troubled by food,' said Chef Asif Quershi, Awadhi specialty chef at the Marriott Hotel, Bhopal, in an interview with the *The Hindu*.[61] This statement captures the entire essence of Awadhi nawabi cuisine.

Lucknow can surprise vegetarians and non-vegetarians alike with its unforgettable offerings. From kebabs to kormas and parathas, food here is created using different combinations of spices to give each dish a distinct character and flavour. Lucknow is also famous for using milk instead of water to cook dishes like the popular biryani from Idris at Raja Bazaar Chowk and for its generous use of ghee. And so I never miss an opportunity to visit the city, trying my best to unearth and discover its many culinary secrets and offerings.

Our hotel was not far from the airport, and in the taxi, my gaze was glued to the view outside. It brought back memories from when I had visited the city as a child. I have always loved pani puri and biryani, and those were among the first dishes I ate when I was in Lucknow the very first time and walked around its old parts. After checking into the hotel, I decided to venture out and explore the city while my friend stayed in to finish work. It was a pleasant day; the weather was cool. I took an auto to the Bada Imambara. After wandering around for a bit, I met a man with a horse-drawn cart who offered to take me around the Bada Imambara and share stories of the place for just ₹50.

Amin Bhai had been riding this cart for 28 years and his horse, Sabrina, had been with him for 20 of those years. His cart was beautifully decorated with plastic pom-poms, postcards of Bollywood actors and had a bright red seat. Sabrina had come from the Pakistan border. Amin Bhai's love for his horse was evident; he spoke to her throughout the ride, placating her when she threw a tantrum. It was a wonderful relationship.

On our way, I spotted a guy selling pani puri and asked Amin Bhai to stop. It is one of my rituals to eat pani puri and chaat in every city that I visit in India, because all of them have a different way of making it. Some mash the potatoes, others dice them, some will add spices and others won't. But in Lucknow, they mash the potatoes, add spices and serve it with tangy tamarind water, and pani puri is called pani batasha, which tastes almost like the ones served in Bihar. Snack break done, Amin Bhai, Sabrina and I continued our ride. When I told Amin Bhai that I'd love to experience the city's rich food culture, as well as go around town as a tourist to photograph it, he got excited and immediately recommended many places where I should eat biryani, kulcha, kebabs and his favourite masala chai. But I was familiar with most of these dishes and places, and so I pressed him for something beyond these well-known Lucknowi offerings. At first he seemed shy and reluctant, but after much pleading he told me I should accompany him to his house and enjoy the special kachori that his wife, Chand Bibi, made. He said it was one of the most amazing dishes in all of Lucknow and that no five-star hotel served it. This offer was right up my alley. There was no way I wasn't going to accept it. '*Chal, Sabrina, aaj thoda jaldi ghar chalte hai, mehman nawazi ka mauka bade dino ke baad mila hai* (Let's go home quickly, Sabrina, today we have a guest),' Amin Bhai urged his companion.

I believe wholesome good food comes from the smallest kitchens. It is often the dishes that were made in households for the simplest of people that have now been transformed into the fancy dishes being served in restaurants today.

We travelled through Ghanta Ghar, which was built in 1881 by Nawab Nasir-ud-Din Haider for the arrival of Sir George Cooper, the first lieutenant governor of the United Provinces of Oudh, and through the colourful streets of Aminabad to Amin Bhai's house, where we were greeted by his wife, Chand Bibi, a woman in her mid-fifties dressed in a light-green sari. I was happy to meet her but I sensed that she was happier, especially since I had brought an appetite. We made ourselves comfortable on a *charpai* with a thin mattress as Chand Bibi fed thin wooden planks into her clay *chulha* and started a fire. She was making kachori, she told me, but not the traditional kind with its regular stuffing of potatoes, onions or lentils. This was different; a recipe she had learned from her mother in Kanpur.

Chand Bibi used some leftover keema from the night before, and mixed in kasuri methi, chaat masala and whole green chillies to enhance the flavour. She kneaded the dough with maida, ghee, milk and water. She told me to fry the kachoris over a low flame, so that the outer layer turned crispy. In almost no time, she served us the crispiest and most beautiful golden-brown kachoris. As I bit into one, the crunch of the outer layer gave way to the flavourful and soft keema inside. She served the kachoris with curd and mango pickle. In a matter of minutes, the plate was wiped clean. We didn't leave a crumb behind. Chand Bibi was kind enough to share the recipe with me and as I was leaving, she smiled proudly and said, '*Ab to aap mera khana* famous *kar doge* (Now you will make my recipe famous).' I promised her I'd try my best.

## Recipe

Serves: 4 to 6

Cooking time: 120 to 140 minutes

**Ingredients**

- 2½ cups all-purpose flour
- Salt to taste
- 1 tbsp oil
- Water as required

***For the keema***

- 250 gm mutton mince
- 1 medium onion, chopped
- ½ tbsp ginger–garlic paste
- 1 tbsp green chilli, chopped
- 2 tsp red chilli powder
- 1 tsp turmeric powder
- 1 tsp cumin powder
- ½ tsp black pepper powder
- ½ tsp garam masala powder
- 1 tsp coriander powder
- Salt to taste
- 2 tbsp fresh coriander, chopped
- 2 tbsp lemon juice
- Oil for frying

**Method**

1. In a deep bowl, add the flour, salt, oil and give it a good mix.
2. Add water, and knead into a soft and firm dough. Cover it with a damp cloth and let it rest for 15–20 minutes.
3. Heat oil in a pan and sauté the onions till they turn translucent.
4. Add the mince and cook it till it turns brown.
5. Toss in the ginger–garlic paste and green chillies and mix well.
6. Add red chilli powder, turmeric, cumin powder, black pepper powder, garam masala powder, coriander powder and salt. Mix well and cook for 10–12 minutes.
7. Add fresh coriander and lemon juice, give it a mix and take it off the flame.

8. Rub a little oil on to your hands and knead the dough once again till it becomes soft. Then let it rest for 5–8 minutes.
9. Divide the dough into equal small balls, put some oil on the rolling board and flatten the dough. Roll out the dough and place the keema filling in the centre of the dough, and seal all edges. Press down gently.
10. In a frying pan, heat oil and fry the kachoris over a low flame until they turn golden brown.
11. Serve hot with chutney and fresh yoghurt.

# 27

# Gulzar Zaidi's Kat-a-Kat

IT WAS LOVE AT first sight. I had never come across a place as simple and beautiful as Amritsar. Even though I was completely at home in this food paradise, I soon came to realize that Amritsar's insatiable appetite could outdo me in a heartbeat. Here people may get tired of eating, but they never get full. Nowadays, when I go to Punjab, I avoid meeting my friends because I can't match their capacity to eat.

A Punjabi's love for food is evident in their language. The insult *'khasama-nu-kha'* literally translates to 'you are so evil, you ate your husband'. My friend Ajay Siotra, a contestant of MasterChef India 2016 and owner of Scootervala in Jammu, told me another phrase – *'Amlay da swad hor budhay lokah dia gallan chiray samjh aundi hai,'* which means, 'It takes time to understand an old man's wisdom and the flavour of gooseberries.' The concept of *'saanjha chulha'* where family members eat and cook in the same kitchen and later eat together on one table still exists to a large extent in this part of the country. I remember, once on MasterChef Vikas Khanna jokingly said, 'The national bird of Punjab is chicken,' and this is definitely true in Amritsar – it is all about *kukkad-shukkar, sharab te kebab* (chicken, booze and kebabs).

Punjabis are also some of the greatest hosts you will ever meet, and especially if you are in Amritsar, they love showing off their rich food culture. When I first visited the city in 2013, my friend Amrit Singh, a student of Khalsa College, took me to the iconic Bharawan da Dhaba and Kesar da Dhaba telling me it would be blasphemy not to visit these two places if I was in the city. Punjabis take pride in their food and he was no different. Both restaurants date back a century and serve authentic vegetarian dishes. At Bharawan da Dhaba I enjoyed their kulchas with chole and a tall glass of lassi, whereas at Kesar da Dhaba I had the thali, which had their iconic palak paneer, dal and chole, and the best phirni I have ever eaten. The dishes served in both places were loaded with ghee, but it still did not feel very heavy on the stomach and, in fact, the ghee enhanced the flavour.

'Punjab' means the land of five rivers; '*panj*' meaning five and '*ab*' meaning waters in Persian. The rivers are the Beas, Sutlej, Chenab, Ravi and Jhelum. Punjab's rich history stems from the fact that it was very strategically placed along the Silk Route. It developed into a major agrarian society producing harvests of wheat, barley, millet, sugarcane, green vegetables and milk, which now largely constitutes the staples of the state's cuisine. The region was raided and occupied by many conquerors over time – Mahmud of Ghazni, Timur, Darius, Alexander of Greece, the Scythians, Turks, Afghans and Mughals. Each of these rulers brought with them their own culture and food, creating an amazingly interesting cuisine. The influence of different Islamic cooking techniques like cooking in a pit, the dum-pukht style, or usage of dry fruit are evident in the food that we eat in Punjab.[59]

Gulzar Zaidi was a person who was affected by Partition in 1947. Gulzar was born in 1927 in Lahore, but lived his entire life on the Indian side of Punjab with his family. Amrit took me to his house in Putligarh, a mere 15 minutes from the Golden Temple. Gulzar Zaidi was a tall man with a wrinkled face, a long white beard and he always wore a skull cap. He had a very deep voice and used a walking stick. He had a knack for meeting new people and hosting them wonderfully in his house. He smelled the way my house smells on the day of Eid – fruity, because of the attar (essential oil).

He told me, he used to live with his extended family in Jhang, Lahore, in a relatively bigger house. During the Partition, Gulzar's extended family packed whatever they could, along with their gold and cash, into a cart, and fled their village. He is not aware of the whereabouts of his extended family now. They kept the gold and cash at hand as collateral to save their lives, in case they encountered a mob. He came to India with his immediate family, simply because his family said they were born in India and they would die in India, and that they'd never be able to relate to this 'new' land. He'd lost touch with everyone, friends in Punjab and family in Lahore. He was teary eyed as he recalled the ugly events of the time. We took a moment's silence to absorb his story, and then Gulzar changed the subject. 'Let's eat now. *Punjabi zada der udaas nahi reh sakte* (Punjabis can't stay sad for too long),' he said.

Zaidi reminded me of Dada. He passed away before I was born, but there were many photographs of him at Fazal Manzil. My parents often told me that Dada enjoyed '*khadi chammach ki* chai' – overtly sweet tea. His cup would have so much sugar in it that the spoon would stand up straight when immersed in it. It turned out that Zaidi, even in his old age, had the same chai. With his permission, I made him my Zaidi Dada.

I was surprised when Zaidi made his wife sit beside him while he began to cook. In all my travels, I'd almost always seen the women of the family in the kitchen. Zaidi liked to cook on special occasions, and if his wife enjoyed the food, it spurred him on to other culinary adventures.

That day, he made kat-a-kat – a Pakistani dish that his Ammijaan would make during Eid. Zaidi Dada sat in front of a small kerosene oil stove, a rare sight today when we have LPG and electric burners. He started pumping the gas into the cylinder that was attached to the stove and after a few minutes asked me to do it. Chote Mamu had a similar blue burner that he would bring along on our picnics. He would always ask the kids to pump the gas after which he'd light up the burner. Doing it again after so many years made me nostalgic, and helped me relive a part of my carefree childhood.

Dada put out an old, flat tawa, big enough to feed at least five to seven people. He peeled some fresh garlic and crushed the cloves roughly before throwing them on the tawa, and then added the innards of the animal, along with a few small pieces of meat and animal fat. In the Islamic tradition, we use every part of the animal; wastage is considered disrespectful to the animal that is slaughtered. Even in Sasaram, during Eid-ul-Zuha, we'd use everything edible, including the fat. The skin of the animal would be donated to a madrasa, which would in turn sell it to leather traders for money for the upkeep of the school. '*Ek baar ye sab bhun jaye fir batata hu, ye* kat-a-kat *kya hai* (Let all of this cook a bit then I'll show you what kat-a-kat is),' he said. Once the meat was cooked and the fat nicely melted, he took out two sharp spatulas and started beating, chopping and mixing everything on the tawa. He added masala and yoghurt, along with some ginger and created a blend. The dish gets its name from the sound of the spatulas on the tawa. After mixing everything together, he let it simmer over a low flame. The reason he first pan-grilled the organs with garlic was to cut out the meat's smell. Turmeric, which has antiseptic properties, is commonly used across India and South East Asia.

We ate the kat-a-kat with fresh tandoori rotis from the nearby market. I ate every morsel on my plate. When I was leaving Zaidi

Dada's house, I realized how little it takes to make good food that you'll never forget – one just needs a few ingredients, conversation and the promise of new friendships.

## Recipe

Serves: 4 to 6

Cooking time: 120 minutes

### Ingredients

- 250 gm mutton chops
- 50 gm mutton kidney (gurdey)
- 50 gm mutton testicles (kapooray)
- 50 gm mutton brain (bheja)
- 2 medium tomatoes, sliced
- 1 large onion, finely chopped, fried
- 3 tsp kat-a-kat masala
- ½ bunch fresh coriander, chopped
- 4 green chillies, chopped
- 2 tbsp ginger–garlic paste
- 2 tbsp garam masala
- 2-inch ginger, julienned
- 1 tsp red chilli powder
- Salt to taste
- 2 tbsp fenugreek leaves (kasuri methi)
- ½ cup thick yoghurt
- 4 tbsp fresh garlic, roughly chopped
- ½ cup ghee/oil
- 2 tbsp turmeric
- ¼ cup of mint leaves

***For the Kat-a-Kat masala***

- 10–12 whole red chillies
- 2 tbsp aniseed (whole)
- 2 tbsp cumin (whole)
- 2 tbsp coriander seeds
- 2 tbsp dry fenugreek (whole)

**Method**

1. Dry roast all the whole spices for the kat-a-kat masala and grind it into a fine powder. Keep aside.
2. Apply salt and the chopped garlic on the kidney and set it aside for 30 minutes. Then wash it properly before cutting it into small pieces.
3. Boil and separate the meat from the mutton chops. The meat should be tender and fall off the bone.
4. Boil the bheja in water and turmeric for 5 minutes, and then discard the veins.
5. In a large pan, toss in the gurdey and kapooray along with the meat. Cook for 10–15 minutes and then break them into small pieces.
6. In the same pan, add the ginger–garlic paste and cook for 5–8 minutes.
7. Toss in the brain, chopped tomato, kat-a-kat masala and red chilli powder. Cover and let it simmer for 10 minutes.
8. Beat the yoghurt and add it into the pan. Top it with fried onion, kasuri methi, garam masala powder and 2 tablespoons of oil. Once again, cover and cook for 10–15 minutes. Adjust the salt.
9. Add the remaining oil, mint, coriander, green chillies and ginger and cook for 5–8 minutes. Serve warm with tandoori roti.

# 28

# Ummi Abdulla's Vendakka Mulakittathu

IT'S BEEN MANY YEARS since I moved to Delhi. Today I know most of the eating haunts, especially in Old Delhi, like the back of my hand. But on one such visit to Nizamuddin, it struck me that I'd almost always eaten non-vegetarian food. Where were the Muslim vegetarian options? I thought back to my college days in Ranchi to the lane where our hostel was, which was dotted with restaurants run by Muslims. There were vegetarian options, but those were limited to dal tadka, paneer, bhindi or soya aloo, which were our staple meals when we were broke. One particular hostel mate always ate meat at these places. His funda was simple – if he was eating out, he would get his money's worth and only eat meat. I hadn't realized that I too had inadvertently adopted his philosophy. Eat vegetables when at home, but not otherwise. Even Ammi makes dal, saag, paneer and other dishes, but none of them seemed traditional. When I asked Ammi if there were any vegetarian dishes that were uniquely Muslim, she laughed and said, 'Paneer tikka.' She's not entirely wrong. Paneer tikka was created as an alternative to chicken tikka, with the introduction of the tandoor to Indian cooking. But paneer tikka is simply an alternative to chicken and not a stand-alone vegetarian dish. But it got me thinking; surely there was some Muslim vegetarian fare somewhere?

One day, a friend pointed me towards the Mappila Muslims of Malabar and their dishes. The Mappila Muslims represent the perfect marriage between Malayali and Islamic traditions. Both these cultures are beautiful and intricate. The origins of Mappila Muslims dates back to the pre-Islamic period, and they are considered the oldest Muslim community in South Asia. According to Hussain Randathani, author of *Mappila Muslims: A Study on Society and Anti Colonial Struggles*, there existed the settlement of pre-Islam in Chaul, Kalyan Supara and Malabar.[63]

Joseph Koyippally Joseph, associate professor at the Central University of Kerala, writes in his journal article, 'Mappila: Identity and Semantic Narrowing', that the word Mappila has many meanings attached to it. The Dravidian meaning of 'Mappila' means bridegroom or son-in-law, but in a regional sense, it also means a child born to an Arab father and a local coastal woman. '*Mappila*': Ma for mother, and *pillai* meaning child's caretaker. There are Jews (Juda Mappila), Syrian Christians (Nazrani Mappila), and the Muslims, historically known as Jonaka Mappila, in Kerala. The community got their name when inter-cultural marriages were taking place, to differentiate themselves from the locals.[64]

Whereas, according to William Logan, author of *Malabar Manual*, 'The word Mappila is a contraction of *maha* [great] and *pilla* [child], honorary title, [as among the Nayars and Christians in Travancore] and it was probably a title of honour conferred on the early Mohammadan immigrants.'[65]

In the seventh century, Arab traders arrived on the Malabar Coast with an eye on its rich spice trade. Soon, they settled down, marrying the locals and sharing with the community their religion, traditions, and culinary practices, thus giving birth to a whole new cuisine. The Jonaka Mappila community's food is similar to the Malabar culinary styles. Abeeda Rasheed, a Calicut native and one of Kerala's best-known home chefs, said in an interview with *Scroll*, 'Different kinds of *pathiris* [rice flour bread], *unnakaya* [a dish made with fried bananas], many kinds of sweets, and most importantly, the biryani are the main components [of Mappila cuisine].'[66] Since Mappila cuisine was born during the spice trade, several dishes are odes to Indian spices. A lot of fried food, like ulli vadas and biryani, is the centre of the dastarkhān.

One unique element about Mappila cuisine is the use of ghee just the way it is used in Arabic and Mughal cuisines. Members of the community often feast together by sitting in a circle and sharing a giant platter that has all sorts of meat and rice dishes. Further digging brought me to Ummi Abdulla's book *Malabar Muslim Cookery*, where she mentions the preparation of vendakka mulakittathu (okra hot curry). It has two basic steps: first, you fry the vendakka (okra) and then cook it in a spicy tamarind gravy. In this dish, apart from coconut oil, there is no usage of coconut in any other form.[67]

One Sunday in August, I decided to attempt this dish. Bhindi (okra) is one of my favourite vegetables and I simply couldn't resist trying this dish. The first time I tried cooking the vegetable was in Ranchi during my college days. But it was a disaster. Neither would the bhindi cook nor was it crispy like I wanted. Frustrated, I rang Ammi up to ask her what I was doing wrong. When she found out that I'd chopped and then washed the bhindi before throwing it into mustard oil with some onions and green chillies, she laughed. That was the day I learned something vital – bhindi is one vegetable that you must first wash and then cut.

I had learned my lesson and would never make the same mistake again. Later, Abbi taught me how to buy fresh bhindi – cracking the tip to test if it is fresh. If it cracks and breaks apart, it means the vegetable is fresh but if it is rigid then it's best to leave it and look for better ones. Clearly, my parents have made me a pro in the art of buying and cooking bhindi.

Using my experience and proficiency in cooking bhindi, I cooked vendakka mulakittathu for my family, asking Ammi to prepare rice. My parents and Shabi are often my guinea pigs for new dishes (though they should feel lucky because this way they get to eat every fancy dish I've ever cooked). I wanted to cook this dish in an earthen pot, which I found at the back of my cupboard, buried behind a pile of all the other utensils and crockery we had. I gave it a wash, and prepared myself by putting on a black apron and sharpening my knife. This time I washed the bhindi first before chopping it. I am one of those people who actually finds chopping vegetables a therapeutic exercise. I chopped them well and started throwing them into the hot pan. I had the cookbook open in front of me so I wouldn't make any mistakes. I wanted to impress everyone at home with this new dish and while my dish was cooking, I called up my Malayali friend, Rashmi, to further enquire about this dish. She said it was first introduced to her by her childhood Muslim friends and later her nani (grandmother) made the same dish, which she ate with matta rice (red rice) and chammanthi podi (powdered chutney). Even when she went abroad for higher studies, she used to miss her nani and this dish the most, so much so that she once made a video call to learn the process step by step.

I asked Ammi to set the table for the food to be served. We sat around the table with some boiled rice, vendakka mulakittathu and papadam. They did enjoy the dish but found it a little too tangy for their taste, which was possibly because north Indian fare tends to be more spicy than tangy. But I became a fan of the cuisine and dish.

However, my hunger to try the real dish did not subside and hence I started seeking out people from the community. I managed to find someone in Bengaluru at a friend's restaurant – Balle Balle Dhaba. I was visiting my friend in December 2018 and he introduced me to one of his chefs, Azan Saleem. Saleem's father was a rickshaw driver and his mother, a housewife. He had my attention from the get-go as I noticed that he cut and washed the okra in a style different from mine. When I asked him about the Mappila Muslim community, he told me that he was from the same community and that his family used to live in Kerala, but that he was born in Bengaluru and had been living there since he was a kid. I was curious about vendakka mulakittathu and his answer made me smile, simply because of the way he said it. He told me that when he was a kid, there was not much that his family could afford and hence, he was brought up on okra; his mother would often make vegetarian dishes that may or may not have had Islamic origins. Eating meat was always an expensive affair and they'd enjoy its flavour only maybe once a month.

I asked Saleem to help me make the real dish after I told him all about my try and what I had learned from Ummi Abdulla's cookbook. We both went into the kitchen and started preparing the food. He first chopped the okra, and asked me to help him with chopping the onions and tomatoes. We lit the stove and started heating the pan and in no time, we were ready with our dish. We picked a small steel plate from the kitchen and put our finished dish directly on it and ate it with boiled rice that was already available. It tasted a little different for multiple reasons: he cooked the okra for longer, which made it much softer than my version, and the tamarind pulp was also on point. I guess when someone native prepares the same dish, they create it in the best way possible because they have likely grown up eating it and know the precise flavour.

I had a flight the very next day and the first thing I cooked that week was vendakka mulakittathu, and this time I was able to recreate the original flavour, which made me wonder how good the non-vegetarian dishes of the Mappila's would be if the vegetarian ones came out so well!

## Recipe

Serves: 2
Cooking time: 45 to 50 minutes

**Ingredients**

- 200 gm ladies' fingers/okra
- 2 pieces tamarind
- 100 gm tomatoes
- 1 large onion
- 4 cloves garlic
- 2 green chillies
- 2 tsp chilli powder
- ½ tsp turmeric powder
- ¼ tsp mustard seeds
- 1 sprig of curry leaves
- 2 tsp oil
- Salt to taste

## Method

1. Wash and pat the okra till they are dry. Cut them into thin, round slices.
2. Soak the tamarind in some warm water.
3. Finely chop the tomatoes, onions and green chillies, and roughly crush the garlic.
4. In a pan, heat the oil and toss in the okra and onion. Sauté till they are lightly browned.
5. Add green chillies, tomato, garlic, chilli powder and turmeric powder and stir well for 2–3 minutes.
6. Add the tamarind extract, sprinkle some water, adjust the salt and let it cook till it is done.
7. In a tadka pan, heat 1 teaspoon of oil and add the mustard seeds till they splutter and curry leaves. Once ready, pour this over the dish and mix well.
8. Serve with steamed rice.

# 29

# Anam Afsha's Vegetable Kurma

MY TRAVEL BUG OFTEN takes me to many exciting places. On my last visit to Chennai I wanted a break from the mundane and hence, decided to seek out the spices and coffee on offer, two of my favourite things.

I was staying with a friend near Mylapore in Chennai, which is a popular place for coffee and one of my favourite brands, Leo Coffee, was started here in 1971. My friend asked me if I wanted to accompany him to Erode, 400 kilometres from where we were staying. He told me that the town is a perfect spot to discover old temples, mosques, churches, natural scenic beauty and handlooms.

I started reading up more and realized that Erode had been ruled by the three major dynasties of south India – the Cheras, Cholas and Pandyas. Later, I learned from *The Flavour of Spice* by Marryam H. Reshii that Erode is also famous for being the land of turmeric.

I packed my small bag and we took a bus to Erode, where we met Anam (my friend's friend), a small trader dealing in herbal beauty products. She was twenty-five, well-educated and lived with her mother, Afsha. Anam's father had left them when she was quite young and it was her mother who had then taken responsibility of the house. Anam had taken her mother's maiden name as her last name, choosing to honour the effort of the woman who had raised her and was always there to support her. Anam started her business to support her mother. She undertook a course to learn how to mix herbal products together to make face creams, soaps and scrubs. To maintain a high quality of production, she imports her ingredients from Germany and has a small mixing machine in her house. I was curious to see and learn the entire process of making beauty products. She picked me up from the bus stop and the first place we stopped at was a small coffee shop. We picked up our glasses and headed to her house. Her house was on the third floor of a blue building and once I entered, I could smell the subtle fragrance of sandalwood.

Anam was a great resource on what to do in Erode and told me about the two popular landmarks – Mahmoodia Masjid and Sri Kongalamman Temple. The mosque was commissioned by the Muslim Welfare Committee and constructed in 1980. It hosts Quran classes and also offers rooms to travellers, and the hall inside is often used for marriage ceremonies. The temple, on the other hand, is ancient, 1,000 years old, and is one of the principal temples of Erode. Local legend is that there were thieves who tried to steal the statue of Kongalamman from the temple because of its beauty and grandiosity, but while they were making away with it, they heard a voice saying they would face the danger and wrath of the goddess. Terrified, they ran away, leaving the statue in Anangur. In the morning, when the villagers found the statue, they built another temple around it and installed the statue in it. Even now, during the chariot festival, all the rituals start in Anangur and go on to Erode. She also said devotees believe that the eight hands of the goddess take away all their challenges and problems.

In the midst of our conversation, Afsha Aunty came out and in her broken Hindi said, '*Tum log baatein hi karoge ya fir khana bhi khaoge* (Are you guys going to keep talking, or will you eat something as well)?' I wasn't expecting this gesture but I obviously couldn't say no to the food. The table was laid out nicely and the food had a distinct, beautiful aroma, different from usual north Indian cuisines. Afsha Aunty had made neer dosa with some vegetable kurma. Usually, Anam would cook the dish, but today, since she was busy with me, her mother had taken over. The kurma had large chunks of pumpkin, carrot and potato, and had been cooked in spices produced in south India, along with coconut milk.

Lizzie Collingham, in *Curry: A Tale of Cooks and Conquerors*, points out that 'kurma' is just another name of 'korma', which finds mention in the *Ain-i-Akbari*, and it also comes under the broader umbrella of curry. Indians claim that 'curry' comes from the Tamil word 'kari', meaning spiced sauce. Although kurma or korma means braising the meat, this dish is traditionally cooked in yoghurt, with spices and dry fruit in the form of a paste over a slow to medium flame for hours to get a fine texture.[67] The tangy flavour comes from the curd, and it gets a thick and silky texture from the dry fruit paste. Bisma Tirmizi records that kurma has central Asian roots, but gained popularity in India during the sixteenth century–Mughal era by the Rajput cooks in Akbar's royal kitchen, under the supervision of Mir Bakawal (one of the nine gems of Akbar's court).[68] Cooking kurma also involves the dum-pukht technique, which was developed in Uttar Pradesh, and it is fascinating to see this fusion between southern and northern cuisine, where the technique is borrowed from the north to cook with southern ingredients.

Anam told me that the food in this region is similar to the food in Chennai and most parts of Tamil Nadu, however one dish that she enjoys the most is katti paruppu, which is a basic and simple dal curry usually prepared with chickpea and very little seasoning. A popular dish in Erode is killu kari, and since it is so famous, it has acquired the name 'Erode killu kari', which essentially is a spicy mutton curry with ginger–garlic paste. Onion and mutton are used in equal proportion in this curry. Although Erode is famous for turmeric (a report in *The Hindu* published in November 2018 that says Erode turmeric occupies about 70 to 75 per cent of the turmeric grown in Erode and Coimbatore districts) it was missing in the kurma I was enjoying.[69] When I asked aunty, she said it was because it dilutes the natural colour of vegetables and the coconut milk and hence she avoids it, though it is a very a common practise in restaurants to add turmeric to everything they cook.

Aunty's kurma was different from the ones north Indians make. If you go to a restaurant in north India, they will always have the option of 'navratan korma', which is very creamy and a little heavy on my stomach. These days restaurants also add a few spoons of the 'kitchen king' spice blend, which is often considered as the 'Ram *baan*' (most effective) for a lot of vegetarian dishes and an inseparable part of the dhaba style of cooking. Navratan translates to nine gems, and the name of the kurma is a hat tip to the cultural inclusion in Akbar's court. Northerners call their version 'korma' and not 'kurma'. Navratan korma has a mix of different flavours and ingredients, including fruit, dry fruit and vegetables. It is safe to assume that perhaps to please the vegetarian diners and guests of the king, royal khansamas introduced this royal delicacy where they used the same technique as a meat korma, braising the ingredients on a high flame and then slow-cooking them in the rich, aromatic gravy. The korma goes well with naan or roomali roti, though the accompaniment depends on personal preference.

This dish prepared by Afsha Aunty had less yoghurt and was prepared in coconut milk along with fresh coconut flesh. I would have asked for naan but she had paired it with neer dosa, which is a very thin and soft dosa. The tangy coconut flavour along with the subtle garam masala and dry fruit paste was mesmerizing for me and each bite was bliss, offering a melt-in-your-mouth experience. I stuffed myself with the amazing food because I realized I would be leaving her house to explore more of Erode, the mosques and temples that Anam talked about, and vowed to buy some of that famous fresh turmeric.

## Recipe

Serves: 4
Cooking time: 45 to 50 minutes

### Ingredients

- 2 pieces tamarind
- 6 whole cashew nuts
- ¼ cup water
- ½ cup potato, chopped
- ½ cup beans, chopped
- ½ cup carrots, chopped
- ½ cup green peas
- ½ cup cauliflower florets
- ½ cup freshly grated coconut
- 2 tbsp coconut oil
- 1½ tbsp channa dal
- 1 tbsp coriander seeds
- 4 dried red chillies

- 1 medium onion, chopped
- 1 big tomato, chopped
- 1 sprig of curry leaves
- 1 tsp mustard seeds
- ¼ tsp asafoetida (hing)
- Salt to taste

**Method**

1. Soak the tamarind and cashews in two separate bowls of warm water for 15 minutes. Strain and keep them aside.
2. Boil all the vegetables for 5–7 minutes (till they turn soft) with a pinch of salt and keep them aside.
3. Take a blender and make a smooth paste out of the soaked cashews and grated coconut.
4. In a pan, heat 1 tablespoon of coconut oil and sauté the channa dal, coriander seeds and dried red chillies for a minute. Then add chopped onions and tomatoes, and sauté again for a few minutes. Allow it to cool down.
5. Grind this in the blender to make a smooth paste.
6. In a heavy-bottomed pan, add the remaining oil, asafoetida and mustard seeds and let it crackle.
7. Add curry leaves and both the pastes with extra water. Cook over a low flame.
8. Once the paste is cooked properly, add tamarind water and let it simmer for a few minutes.
9. Adjust the salt and mix in all the boiled vegetables.
10. Let the dish cook for a few minutes in the gravy. Adjust the consistency as per your choice.
11. Serve with steamed rice.

# 30

# Ruwangan Tchaaman

DURING MY STINT ON MasterChef in 2016, one of the challenges required us to cook with saffron. To be very honest, I was anxious about it. I have never found any distinct flavour in saffron. Perhaps it was because my family used so little of it or because its flavour gets overpowered by the other ingredients of a dish. I have seen Ammi using saffron, but only in small quantities. I think she mostly used it for the luxurious colour. I have also seen the naanbais of Sasaram and Delhi use saffron in sheermal, bakarkhani and other breads, but once again, I had never been able to isolate the flavour of saffron from the rest of the dish. And so I was anxious about this challenge. I made seviyan biryani (vermicelli biryani) with butterbeans and a few other vegetables. I added saffron and it gave me the desired colour, but I was still unsure about the flavour and thus nervous about the result. Chef Vikas, Chef Kunal and Zorawar Sir liked the overall taste and presentation of my dish, but they all raised the same issue: 'Sadaf, *saffron ka flavour kam hai* (We can't taste the saffron).' I went back to my station, already planning my next move to ensure I could stay at the top of my game in the competition.

Sharanya Deepak, an independent journalist, shared her saffron story with me, telling me that in Kashmir, saffron is a carefully used commodity since people are aware of how precious it is. When I stay at my friend Dr Musharraf Masoodi's in Ganderbal, she shows me how she infuses saffron into dishes for special occasions, even growing her own to add into kahwa (tea) and dishes with paneer, and also in her own home-spun pulao recipe. To her, like many others, saffron is not a matter of taste but an indication of ceremony, an aura of celebration that is created through it.

Almost a year after the show aired, I was asked by a journalist from an online news portal to talk about saffron, and once again, I was reminded of my woes with this mystery ingredient. Saffron is a key ingredient in Kashmiri food, a cuisine I have always found a little complicated and think I won't be able to do justice to. Sharanya Deepak talks about the history of saffron in an article: '... There are many local legends about how saffron came to Kashmir. One goes back to the twelfth century, and says that Sufi saints Khawaja Masood Wali and Sheikh Sharif-ud-din Wali presented a local chieftain with a saffron bulb after he cured them of an illness while they were traveling. Other claims that the Persians brought it in 500 BCE, as a means to further trade and market.'[70] *Buddhist Sects and Sectarianism* by Bibhuti Baruah gives an alternate story. According to Baruah, ancient Chinese history mentions Indian Buddhist missionary Madhyantika, who sowed Kashmir's first saffron crop when he was sent to Kashmir in the fifth century BCE. Saffron went on to become the official colour of Buddhist robes and mantles immediately after the death of Buddha.[71] Another snippet of folklore I heard most recently was that saffron came to Kashmir in the eleventh and twelfth centuries CE with sufis Khwaja Masood Wali and Hazrat Sheikh Shariffudin. There seems to be no proof of this, but it is quite interesting to see how even something as simple as a spice has so many stories behind it.

Saffron has many names in various Indian languages. It is kunkuma (Tamil), zaffran (Urdu), kesar (Hindi), kong (Kashmiri) or kungumapu (Malayalam). The Kashmir Valley is a prominent cultivation point for saffron due to its cool, dry climate and rich soil. Since growing saffron is labour intensive, it is widely noticed that the families that grow saffron are usually big, reducing the cost they would otherwise incur by hiring labour.

While, I was doing my research on saffron, sitting at the Khoj Canteen in Khirki, New Delhi, a tall, fair guy approached me and asked me what I was doing. Puzzled by his curiosity, I told him I was looking up information about saffron. He introduced himself as Ali, a resident of Khirki, and told me that he was an artist and dancer. I realized I had seen him around the neighbourhood, but had never spoken to him before. He started talking about food and told me how his grandmother would use saffron in almost everything, irrespective of whether the dish needed it or not. It was her favourite spice.

Upon hearing all this, I asked him about the major differences between Kashmiri Muslim and Hindu food. He told me that Brahmins and Pandits in Kashmir enjoy meat, but, unlike the Muslims, they don't add onion and garlic in their food.

Colleen Sen writes that the 'preferred meat in the Valley is goat – the younger the better. It is to be marinated in yoghurt and spices and cooked with milk and cream to produce a rich and thick sauce. One of the most popular dishes not just in Kashmir but outside as well is dum aloo, small potatoes cooked in yoghurt and spices to perfection.'

Kashmiris and Bengalis have many similarities in their cuisine. Both use mustard oil to cook their food and the dining table will often find place for non-vegetarian dishes. The cold weather means that Kashmiris rely on meat as their source of protein and energy. Ali told me that they have been blessed with so many varieties of fresh fruit, turnips and vegetables that they try and use this produce in their regular food. Then, he told me about a paneer dish that intrigued me because I had never heard about it before. The traditional name of the dish is 'ruvangan tchaaman', which literally translates to 'paneer with tomatoes'. All this talk about food was making me hungry. Ali got the recipe for the dish from his mother and I decided to give it a try.

We exchanged numbers and I promised I'd make him the dish – it probably wouldn't be as good as his grandmother's version, but I would give it an honest try. He smiled and suggested that I should add some roasted saffron to give it a beautiful colour and flavour. I didn't have the heart to tell him I didn't know what saffron's true flavour was like. But I was excited to have made a new friend and to try a recipe handed down by his grandmother.

Back home, I got some paneer to try out the new recipe. A great way of adding body to a paneer dish is by frying it before adding it to the gravy. Ammi does it all the time, and all her paneer dishes are delicious. In my dish, the flavour of saunf (fennel seeds) was quite nice, which is true for a lot of Kashmiri dishes but the introduction of saffron in the dish gave it a beautiful golden colour and added to the natural red gravy. I was also told to enjoy the dish with butter naan and pickled onion. But I ordered some warm, fresh naan and did not really add all the suggested accompaniments. Even then, it tasted delicious. It is dishes like these that give flavour to the Kashmiri dastarkhān.

Chef Nalini Sadhu, owner of Matamaal restaurant in Gurugram, told me that this is the only vegetarian dish cooked in a traditional *tarami* (copper dish). The reason for adding paneer and not turnip or saag is simply because other things cannot compete with the luxury and richness of meat. All the dishes are cooked in mustard oil without cream or any other kind of fattening agent, which for me was an interesting take, because often people say that a dish from a Muslim kitchen ought to have cream and lots of spices for a rich and luxurious texture.[72]

She further added, that there is a possibility that ruvangan tchaaman originated in a Muslim kitchen because of the use of onion and garlic in the dish. I asked Marryam H. Reshii to confirm this and she agreed; the dish is the de facto vegetarian dish at a *wazwan* (Kashmiri multi-course meal).

Chef Sadhu also said that she feels the real flavour of the dish is dying because of our new-age fast-cooking techniques. Many people who make Kashmiri food will use quick fix masalas, and cheap oil and fat instead of mustard oil. When I asked her if she thinks people use 'kitchen king' masala in their dishes for that reason (the most basic and default spice mix that is used at most small-scale Indian restaurants), she agreed and said they probably do, because they must serve their food quickly and make money. When you use these spice mixes, it just does not pay enough respect to the original dish.

I feel Kashmiri food gets its unique flavour from the precision in the spices used and the techniques applied in the cooking. For example, in ruvangan tchaaman, the flavours emanate from the primary ingredients, tomato and paneer, and nothing else. Often, it is the simple dishes that are the most delicious.

My ruvangan tchaaman also has a touch of saffron in it, which gives it a beautiful colour. Traditionalists may reject my dish, or if I'm lucky, it'll gain currency because of the degree of luxury the saffron adds to it. After making this dish and adding a few extra strands of saffron, I learned that perhaps the flavour of saffron was a little metallic and rustic, and that it added a royal colour to my dish. I still won't call myself a saffron expert, but I think I now have a fair bit of information about this mystery ingredient.

---

## Recipe

Serves: 2 to 4
Cooking time: 40 to 45 minutes

### Ingredients

- 300 gm paneer
- 6 tbsp mustard oil
- 7 green cardamoms
- 4 brown cardamoms
- 2 bay leaves
- 2 cinnamon sticks
- 1½ cups tomato puree
- ¼ tsp dry ginger powder
- 1 tsp red chilli powder
- 1 tbsp saunf (fennel) powder
- 1 cup water
- A pinch of asafoetida (hing)
- Salt to taste
- A few roasted strands of saffron in warm milk

### Method

1. Cut the paneer into big cubes.
2. In a pan, add 4 tablespoons oil, and shallow fry the paneer pieces till they turn light brown. Keep them aside in warm water mixed with salt and hing.

3. In a separate deep pan, add the remaining oil and turn the flame to high, till the oil smokes. Add the brown cardamoms, green cardamoms, bay leaves and cinnamon, and cook till it splutters.
4. Toss in the dry ginger powder with the tomato puree, salt and red chilli powder. Cook on a low flame till the oil separates from the masala.
5. Add the paneer pieces into the masala.
6. Sprinkle the saunf powder and mix gently.
7. Pour the saffron milk into the gravy
8. Add water into the gravy and mix well.
9. Cover and cook for another 2 minutes.
10. Serve with steamed rice.

31

# Culmination

WHEN I WAS FINISHING this book, someone asked me how much travel and meeting people had influenced my adventures with food – both for my stint on MasterChef in 2016, and in life after that.

The question prompted a look back at my days in school. I was a student at Dayanand Anglo Vedic (DAV) school and one tradition of the institution was to host a havan (a Hindu ritual) every Saturday. At the end of the havan, we would get channa (peanut) and mishri (rock sugar) as prasad (offering). I would often sit in the front row or next to our teacher, chanting the mantras and in the end take the plate of prasad from him to distribute to my classmates. However, my only motive in this act of kindness was to eat more of the prasad. In many ways the memory of that habit embodies my relationship with food – there is a time to share and a time to relish it while by your lonesome.

This book is a recounting of my food journey and my sincere wish was to take my readers on the same journey with me. I had come across numerous dishes on my travels, but these 30 recipes were selected because they are associated with fond memories – either of the people who introduced me to them or the place I encountered them in.

The idea of writing this book and the concept came simply because Muslim food is what I have grown up eating and am most comfortable with. The variety by which one can cook the same dish is amazing and is seen even within my own family – be it my mother, aunts, cousins or uncles. All of them have a different way and take on making similar kinds of food. For example, when my family makes Bihari kebabs, my mother prefers slicing the meat thinly and getting a deep char mark, whereas my aunts focus their energy on the mince mix. Some add more spices and the others less, but the end goal is always to serve a dish that has a balanced flavour.

Moreover, the development of this book has been a steep learning curve for me with regard to my culture and the many facets of Islamic culture in India. Before compiling these recipes, if someone had asked me the major influences of Islamic traditions on Indian cuisine, I would most likely have drawn a blank. I have grown since then and I am in a better position to talk from a place of understanding about the matter. It can be said that Islamic traditions gave a new twist to the food that already existed in the country. The beauty of Indian cuisine is, of course, the multiple cultures it draws from. Islamic traditions are but one source of influence. We should equally credit Portuguese, French and other cultures for bringing in their cooking methods and shaping the dishes that we now popularly call Hindustani *khaana*.

While I was writing this book, people had their own versions of food recipes to narrate. A few were 'authentic' whereas others were passed down over generations. One of the dishes I was writing about was korma from Rampur. Many recipes as well as experts instructed that one must add tomatoes, whereas later, when I enquired more, I realized that the real Rampuri korma asked only for whisked yoghurt. Surprisingly, the food that we eat, talk about and take pride in are also the most under-explored with respect to background research. There are multiple conflicting stories about whether the 'dopiaza' dish is named after Mullah Dopiaza, if it was indeed a favourite dish of the Mullah or if it was simply because the dish is cooked with onions at two different stages. Despite my research, I am still unclear and hence, presented all the different back stories in this book. Many of these stories could very well be folklore, but that only added to the charm of this whole project.

This struggle to find the story behind dishes made me realize how easy it is for food stories to die out. I also came to the realization that in some ways, this project allowed for an evolution of the lore surrounding a dish. Just as spice mixes have changed hands and have seen alterations in their make-up as well as usage, food and the stories surrounding it seem to branch out based on the palate of home cooks and chefs. I still consider myself a novice simply because of the vastness of our country and the range of dishes that we have. It is, in my opinion, almost impossible for a person to know everything.

As a chef, researcher and storyteller, I have realized how important it is to have an overlap between all these three professions. I started writing because I realized that largely everyone can cook, but not everyone has admission to well-researched material, or the prose to interpret that material. Since I had the ability for both, I thought I would exploit it.

More than just documentation, there is a need for such material to be accessible to everyone. I have great respect for people like Dr Pushpesh Pant, Dr Ashish Chopra, Dr Mohsina Mukadam, Jiggs Kalra, Grand Chef Imtiaz Qureshi, Lizzie Collingham, Rushina Munshaw Ghildiyal, Salma Husain and others like them, who have spent a fair bit of their lives in finding out the history of food and keeping the romance alive, by celebrating the culinary differences of the country as well as the evolved culinary culture and traditions.

I hope that having read my narrative, my readers would now be more inclined to not just eat but also respect Hindustani tradition. I encourage all my readers to ask after food, enjoy the stories that will pop up around them and marvel at the inspirations behind each dish, while they enjoy its flavours. As I finish this last chapter, I am already planning my next trip and the kind of food I will enquire after, fully ready to continue documenting my stories through my blog and video content. Irrespective of the medium, one thing I have learned is that it is important to document the narrative or else, as my college teacher once told me, 'Jungle *mein more nacha, kisne dekha* (Who will notice the peacock dancing in the jungle if you don't spread the word)?'

Food journeys are enchanting, and if you mix food with travel and culture, you expose yourself to the different layers that compose a people. Hence, keep eating, keep exploring.

# Appendix

## Green Chutney (Dhaniya Chutney)

The following is the recipe for the coriander 'green' chutney that many of the dishes are paired with.

---

### Recipe

**Ingredients**

- 250 gm dhaniya (coriander leaves)
- 2 medium sized tomatoes
- 2–3 green chillies
- 2–3 cloves of garlic
- 1 inch of ginger
- 1 tsp cumin seeds
- ½ tsp amchur (dry mango powder)
- Salt to taste
- 1–2 tsp juice of a lemon
- Water as required

## Method

1. Wash and clean the coriander leaves, tomatoes and green chillies. Chop them into small pieces and blend them in a mixer grinder.
2. Put all the remaining ingredients together in the same blend. Adjust water to give it the desired consistency
3. Grind into a smooth paste.
4. The chutney is ready to be served.

# Notes


1. Chitrita Banerji, *Eating India*. New Delhi: Penguin India, 16 January 2008.
2. Podcast by Shaykh Hamza Yusuf on islamveg.com
3. Vinod Chandra Srivastava , ed. *History of Agriculture in India, Up to C. 1200* AD. Concept Publishing Company, 2008.
4. Bibhu Prasad Singh and Rajesh K. Rana, 'History of Potato and its Emerging Problems in India', Indian Potato Association, January 2014.
5. K.T. Achaya, *A Historical Dictionary of Indian Food*. New Delhi: Oxford University Press, 28 November 1998.
6. Jessica Lynn, 'Where Are The Most Potatoes Grown?'. 25 April 2017. Accessed from https://www.worldatlas.com.
7. Annemarie Schimmel, *The Empire of the Great Mughals: History, Art and Culture*. Reaktion Books, 1 October 2004.
8. Devdutt Pattanaik, *Jaya: An Illustrated Retelling of the Mahabharata*. Penguin India, 16 August 2010.
9. 'The Two-Onion Mystic & Nine Gems'. 8 September 2013. Accessed from https://kitchensofhistory.wordpress.com.
10. *Nimmatnama-i Nasiruddin-Shahi*, A Medieval Indian Cookbook, written in the Nastalīq script, of delicacies and recipes, and some accompanying paintings illustrating the preparation of the recipes. It was started for Ghiyath al -Din Khalji (r. 1469–1500), the ruler of the Malwa Sultanate in central India. After he was forced to

abdicate, it was completed for his son Abd al-Muzaffar Nasir Shah. (r. 1500–10).

11. Sumit Paul, 'How Kolkata Got Its Parantha'. *The Hindu*, 15 November 2014.
12. Kalyan Karmakar, 'The Mysterious Story of Kolkata's Moghlai Paratha'. 13 May 2016. Accessed from https://www.finelychopped.net.
13. Bisma Tirmizi, 'Food Stories: Bihari Kabab'. *Dawn*, 25 September 2015.
14. *Rihlat Ibn Battuta* (*Travels of Ibn Battuta*), Ibn Battuta. Dar Al Koutoub Al Alamia, 2014.
15. S.S. Prasad on the Epic Channel show *Raja, Rasoi aur Anya Kahaniya*, Season 2, episode 17, February 2016.
16. Deblina Chakravorty, 'Nihari, a gift from Nawabs'. *Times of India*, 12 April 2012.
17. Sadia Dehlvi, *Jasmine and Jinns: Memories and Recipes of My Delhi*. Harper Collins, July 2017.
18. Anvar Alikhan, 'Roll Model'. *Outlook*, 5 May 2008.
19. Jaideep Mazumdar, 'From Puchkas To Parathas And Kebabs: Food Aplenty On Kokalta's Streets'. *Swarajya*, 29 July 2018.
20. Bisma Tirmizi, 'Food Stories: Murgh Musallam'. *Dawn*. 30 June 2014.
21. Colleen Taylor Sen, *Feasts and Fasts: A History of Food in India*. London: Reaktion Books, 2015.
22. Anoothi Vishal, 'Murgh Musallam: The Extravagant Stuffed Whole-Chicken Dish'. NDTV Food, 9 March 2018.
23. Digvijaya Singh, *Cooking Delights Of The Maharajas*. Vakils Feffer and Simons, 1982.
24. Sanchari Pal, 'Food Fit for Royalty: So What Did The Mughal Emperors Eat For Dinner?'. The Better India, 31 August 2018.
25. Ankit Chadha, *Amir Khusrau: The Man in Riddles*. Gurugram: Penguin Random House India, 2016.
26. Rana Safvi, 'All about Paan, Paandaan and Paan Kharch'. 14 January 2016. Accessed from: http://ranasafvi.com

27. Madhulika Dash, 'Diwali, a festival for Delhi Sultans'. *Hindustan Times.* 23 November 2015.
28. Dr Indu Mehta, 'Origin and History of Onions'. *IOSR Journal of Humanities And Social Science,* Vol 22, Issue 9, September 2017.
29. Alan Davidson, *The Oxford Companion to Food.* New York: Oxford University Press, 1999.
30. Margaret Shaida, *The Legendary Cuisine of Persia,* London: Grub Street, 2000.
31. Annia Ciezadlo, 'History on a Plate'. *Time,* 21 July 2011.
32. Bismi Tirmizi, 'Food Stories: Haleem'. *Dawn,* 11 November 2014.
33. Amrita Roy, 'The original slow food staple'. *Livemint,* 10 September 2010.
34. Dr Manas Kumar Das, 'History of Odisha (From 1435 TO 1803 A.D.)'. Bhubaneswar: DDCE, Utkal University. Accessed from http://ddceutkal.ac.in.
35. Vikram Doctor, 'India's food politics and how it was capable of caste promotion'. *Economic Times,* 28 October 2018.
36. Madhulika Dash, 'Italy wants its pizza to be on a global cultural heritage list. Which Indian dish should find a place on it?', *Indian Express,* 1 April 2016.
37. Laura Siciliano-Rosen, 'Chicken tikka masala'. Encyclopaedia Britannica Inc., 22 October 2014.
38. Soity Banerjee, 'Cooking the world's oldest known curry'. BBC India, 22 June 2016.
39. Arunima Kashyap and Steve Weber date the discovery of curry to between 2500BCE and 2200BCE, Washington State University, Vancouver.
40. Madhulika Dash, 'Food Story: The Saga of Mirch Ka Salan'. *Indian Express,* 22 January 2015.
41. Shashank Angiras, 'Eat Like Royalty: A Look Inside The Royal Kitchens Of Rampur'. 17 January 2018. Accessed from https://eattreat.in.

42. Madhulika Dash, 'The rise and revival of the ancient Rampuri cuisine'. *Indian Express*, 18 September 2014.
43. Pratibha Karan, *Biryani*. Gurugram: Penguin Random House India, 26 July 2017.
44. Sunil Kumar, D. C. Rai, K. Niranjan, and Zuhaib F. Bhat, 'Paneer—An Indian soft cheese variant: a review', *Journal of Food Science & Technology*, 26 October 2011.
45. John Clark Marshman, *History of India: From the Earliest Period to the Close of Lord Dalhousie's Administration*, 1929. Accessed from Archives.org.
46. Anwar Ali Khan on The Epic Channel show *Lost Recipes* on Kursi miyana.
47. 'Khajuraho Temples'. *Khajuraho India*. Accessed from https://khajuraho-india.org.
48. Bisma Tirmizi, 'Food Stories: Karhi'. *Dawn*, 14 April 2015.
49. K.T. Achaya, *Indian Food: A Historical Companion*. New Delhi: Oxford University Press, 1994.
50. Shaharyar M. Khan, *The Begums of Bhopal: A History of the Princely State of Bhopal*. I.B. Tauris, 28 July 2000.
51. Joanna Lobo, 'Kolkata's best versions of Rezala'. *Times of India*, 8 June 2014.
52. Marryam H. Reshii, *The Flavour of Spice: Journeys, Recipes, Stories*. Gurugram: Hachette India, 2017.
53. Monish Gujral , *On the Kebab Trail: A Moti Mahal Cookbook*. Gurugram: Penguin Random House India, 2013.
54. Digital Dictionaries of South Asia. Accessed from https://dsal.uchicago.edu.
55. Usha R. Prabhakaran, *Usha's Pickle Digest*. Self-published, 1998.
56. Usha R. Prabhakaran, 'Spice up your meal'. *The Hindu*, 30 April 2000.
57. Bisma Tirmizi, 'Food Stories: Achar Ghost'. *Dawn*, 7 April 2015.
58. Lizzie Collingham, *Curry: A Tale of Cooks and Conquerors*. London: Vintage Books, 2006.

59. Izzat Husain, *Izzat Ka Khana: Mughlai Cuisine Recipes*. Notion Press, Inc, 2018.
60. J. Inder Singh Kalra and Pradeep Das Gupta, *Prashad: Cooking with Indian Masters*. Allied Publishers Pvt Ltd, 1986.
61. Shilpa Nair Anand, 'Food of the Nawabs'. *The Hindu*, 7 May 2018.
62. *Turko-Persia in Historical Perspective*, Ed. Robert L. Canfield. Cambridge: Cambridge University Press, 2002.
63. Hussain K. Randathani, *Mappila Muslims: A Study on Society and Anti Colonial Struggles*. Calicut: Other Books. 2007.
64. Joseph Koyippally Joseph, '"Mappila": Identity and semantic narrowing'. *IOSR Journal of Humanities and Social Science*, Vol 22, Issue 1, Ver 6, January 2017.
65. William Logan, *The Malabar Manual*. 1867. Victoria Institutions, 2018.
66. Sharanya Deepak, 'Why Kerala's Mappila cuisine needs evangelists like Abida Rasheed'. *Scroll*, 5 May 2018.
67. Ummi Abdulla, *Malabar Muslim Cookery*. New Delhi: Orient BlackSwan, 1993.
68. Bisma Tirmizi, *Feast: With a Taste of Amir Khusro*. New Delhi: Rupa Publications, 2017.
69. Sanjay Vijayakumar , 'Registry accepts application for Erode Turmeric GI Tag'. *The Hindu*, 8 November 2018.
70. Sharanya Deepak , 'This Land Is Meant Only for Saffron. Without It, It Means Nothing.' *Eater*, 13 February 2019. Accessed from https://www.eater.com.
71. Bibhuti Baruah, *Buddhist Sects And Sectarianism*. New Delhi: Sarup & Sons, 2000.
72. Interview with Chef Nalini Sadhu in December 2018.

# Acknowledgements

Any project requires a team, a well-oiled machine with different parts performing different functions to ensure the smooth completion of a project.

To finish this book, I had to consult a lot of people, friends, food lovers, experts, family members, chefs, cooks and practically every other person I saw eating food on the streets. All of them had suggestions to make and I am deeply thankful for every bit of one of them. I was able to chance upon a lot of ideas and worked on most, if not all, of them.

I had an urge to share my love for food with the world and show it to people in ways that went beyond cooking. I thought of marrying my love for food, research, writing and storytelling together, and came up with this book. My initial discussion started with Manasi Bose, who first helped streamline the many ideas I had, and then burned the midnight oil going through all the chapters and making them look beautiful. She also had to experience first-hand, and handle, my madness as I worked on this endeavour by going through my chapters one at a time and giving her creative inputs and feedback. Once the draft pitch was ready, it was time to share it with Ammi, Abbi and Shabi. After all, it was going to be the story of the Hussain clan. Throughout my writing, they helped with the content and answered all my relevant (and not so relevant) questions. Once, I was ready with all the pieces of this puzzle, it was time to pitch it and find publishers. While I was running from pillar to post to find connections in publishing houses, Vidushi Sabharwal came to my rescue and helped me connect with Hachette India.

I would also like to acknowledge all the people whom I met during my food expeditions, starting from my childhood days till date. It was lovely to reminisce about the wonderful times I had with friends whom I had met at different points of my life. Most don't realize how they have shaped my life and each chapter is dedicated to all of those unsung heroes. This list is to include all the other characters including my lovely family, friends and food mentors that you have met in the chapters.

If I look back, I can actually claim that the success and compilation of this book goes to all the ladies I have met and worked with throughout the process. I can't thank Anshika Varma enough for capturing the beautiful cover picture and patiently hearing out all my random demands made at different points of time; Trisha Bora for working on the language, asking me all the right questions and making me work on the parts that were not obvious; Ansila Thomas for coordinating the whole project, listening to my rants and laughing at my not-so-funny jokes; and Poulomi Chatterjee for being the anchor who pulled us all together. I must also acknowledge Prerna Vohra with whom I started this project in the beginning. It was she who liked my concept note and gave me a green flag to begin with.

This book is not the effort of just one person but is the fruit of the collective labour of everyone who handled my insanity as I wove together *Daastan-e-Dastarkhān*.

